W9-CEZ-596

AMTRAK

Explorations in Public Policy

Series Editor
James J. Gosling, University of Utah

AMTRAK

The History and Politics of a National Railroad

David C. Nice

LYNNE
RIENNER
PUBLISHERS

BOULDER
LONDON

Published in the United States of America in 1998 by
Lynne Rienner Publishers, Inc.
1800 30th Street, Boulder, Colorado 80301

and in the United Kingdom by
Lynne Rienner Publishers, Inc.
3 Henrietta Street, Covent Garden, London WC2E 8LU

Library of Congress Cataloging-in-Publication Data
Nice, David C., 1952–
   Amtrak : the history and politics of a national railroad / David
C. Nice.
      p.   cm. — (Explorations in public policy)
      Includes bibliographical references and index.
      ISBN 1-55587-734-6 (hardcover : alk. paper)
      1. Amtrak—History. 2. Railroads—United States—Passenger
traffic—History. 3. Railroads—Government policy—United States—
History. I. Series.
HE2791.A563N53   1998
385'.22'0973—dc21   97-37756
                                                                                                 CIP

British Cataloguing in Publication Data
A Cataloguing in Publication record for this book
is available from the British Library.

Contents

Tables

Preface

We seem to be afflicted with a chronic desire to be on the move. The urge to travel is reflected not only in the immense amount of traveling that U.S. citizens in particular do each year but also in many aspects of popular culture. Travel is a prominent theme in many movies, books, and magazines; an entire cable television channel is devoted to the topic.

Transportation policies profoundly influence daily life, including matters as basic as access to employment opportunities and the ability to travel in reasonable safety and comfort. From a broader perspective, transportation policies affect the quality of the environment, the functioning of the economy, and a nation's dependence on foreign energy sources.

Although transportation policies have generally not been as controversial in the United States as issues such as welfare or taxes, some transportation programs, such as Amtrak, seem to be constantly embroiled in conflict. In this study, I will explore a number of the issues that face the Amtrak system.

• • •

I have been doing research on Amtrak for approximately fifteen years; this book draws on a number of studies completed during that time. I thank the following journals for permission to use materials from these articles: "The States and Passenger Rail Service," *Transportation Research* 21A (1987): 385–390 (with kind permission from Elsevier Science Ltd., The Boulevard, Langford Lane, Kidlington OX5 1GB, UK); "Program Survival and Termination: State Subsidies of Amtrak," *Transportation Quarterly* 42 (1988): 571–585; "Stability of the Amtrak System," *Transportation Quarterly* 43 (1989): 557–570; "Service Distribution on a National Scale: The Case of Amtrak," *Polity* 23 (1991): 487–503; "Passenger Train Ridership in the Amtrak System," *Transportation Quarterly* 45 (1991): 121–132; "Financial Performance of the Amtrak System," *Public Administration*

Review 51 (1991): 138–144; "International Amtrak Service," *Transportation Quarterly* 46 (1992): 619–629; and "Passenger Rail Service: Decline and Resurgence," *Transportation Quarterly* 50 (1996): 95–106.

I am also grateful to everyone at Lynne Rienner Publishers, especially to my editors, Dan Eades and Don Reisman, for their guidance and assistance, and to Cathy Hamilton and Lynne Rienner.

Lisa Janowski provided invaluable assistance with word processing and caught a number of mistakes that I had overlooked.

Finally, my most important thanks go to my wife, Ruth, who has been an unfailing source of encouragement and support. I dedicate this book to her.

David C. Nice

AMTRAK

1

Creating Amtrak

Transportation is one of the most basic responsibilities of governments in the United States. Public programs supported the initial construction of much of the nation's railroad system, the building of nearly all of the nation's roads and highways, the development of the air transportation system, and the construction of many of the facilities and routes used for water transportation. Government regulations have significantly affected all of the major transportation modes to one degree or another, and government funding has supported much of the research to develop new transportation technologies. No significant aspect of the transportation system has escaped the influence of public policies.

The U.S. transportation system has changed substantially since World War II. The construction of the Interstate Highway System greatly enhanced the appeal of road transportation, both for passengers and freight. Air travel became the dominant public carrier mode for intercity passenger travel. In addition, the national government found itself in the passenger train business.

Early in U.S. history, passenger travel was often difficult and uncomfortable. People walked or traveled by horse, generally on dirt roads. Travelers along the coast could go by boat, an option that was also available on some rivers and, later, on canals. With the coming of the railroads, people gained the ability to travel farther and faster than most had ever imagined. Although the early passenger trains were not very comfortable, track and equipment gradually improved. The railroads helped to link different sections of the country and speeded the settlement of the western United States.

The railroads were among the first big businesses in the United States, and major railroad executives became celebrities. By 1900, a traveler on a first-class train could expect to find good food, a library, a barber shop, and the company of prominent individuals from the worlds of business, politics, and entertainment. Passenger trains appeared in a wide range of

1

popular art forms—in cheap books about train robbers, in Broadway shows, and in many movies, including *Union Pacific, Strangers on a Train,* and *North by Northwest.* The passenger train for a time appeared to occupy a secure place in society.

Decline of the Passenger Train

The 1920s, however, saw the beginning of a long-term decline in U.S. passenger train service, a decline that continued, with a major interruption during World War II, through the 1960s. For example, in the late 1920s, the United States had approximately twenty thousand passenger trains in service. By 1970, only 450 remained, and roughly 100 of them were in the process of being discontinued. In 1929, the United States had more than two hundred thousand miles of passenger train routes. By 1966, that figure had fallen by more than two-thirds.[1] Many communities that were served by several trains daily and by more than one railroad in the 1920s found that they were served by a single train or none at all by the 1960s.

Passenger volume also declined dramatically. The number of passenger miles traveled by train fell by nearly 80 percent from 1920 to 1970, and the proportion of travelers going by train rather than by other modes fell even more.[2] This emerging pattern led to three questions. Why was the decline occurring? What consequences would it have? And what, if anything, should be done about it? Here, as in the case of many public policies, differing perceptions of the nature of the problem led to differing views regarding the most appropriate response.[3]

The Causes of Decline

One of the most widely cited causes for the decline of passenger trains is the degree of financial loss that they incurred. As early as the late 1930s, passenger trains were losing over $200 million annually. After World War II, the losses increased to a high of over $700 million in 1957, then declined to approximately $400 million annually during the 1960s.[4] Few private-sector activities can endure financial losses of that magnitude for very long.

Not all observers accept the thesis that financial losses caused the decline of passenger trains. Failing to distinguish between the costs of facilities used by both passenger and freight trains created opportunities for inflating apparent passenger train costs, and genuine losses on some routes may have given the railroads an incentive to overstate passenger train losses overall in order to gain approval for abandoning those routes. According to this view, the apparent passenger train deficit was simply a fiction of bookkeeping.[5]

While this controversy is difficult to resolve conclusively, the weight of the evidence points to a few conclusions. First, several different estimation methods all indicate that passenger trains were in fact losing money after World War II. Second, the estimated magnitude of the losses varies considerably. Third, financial losses seem to be widespread not only for passenger trains all across the United States but also for rail travel in many other countries.[6] Overall, financial losses are one plausible reason for the decline of passenger rail service but not necessarily the only reason. Other factors may have contributed to the decline and to the financial losses as well.

✦ Perhaps the most prominent of those factors is technology. Improvements in automobile design and highway engineering have given automobile travel a convenience and flexibility that railroads have been unable to match and that travelers and commuters in most locales seem to rely on, even with attendant traffic jams and parking shortages. Improvements in aircraft and flight control systems have given the airlines a tremendous speed advantage over trains on long-distance trips. Passenger trains, in this view, represent an outmoded technology that has been pushed aside by other transportation modes offering consumers a better value.[7]

The technological explanation is extremely important for determining an appropriate response to the passenger train's decline. If the passenger train is simply obsolete, then market forces are weeding out an option that is no longer needed. If this view is correct, public policies should focus on making the elimination of passenger trains as smooth as possible. Policies designed to preserve passenger rail service will not be cost effective.

The technological status of any transportation mode, however, is subject to change. For example, airplanes can maintain their speed advantage only if abundant quantities of petroleum fuels are available. Furthermore, new generations of passenger trains now offer the promise of higher speeds—perhaps exceeding 250 miles per hour—that could be more competitive with air travel on short to intermediate distances and offer greater competition to automobiles on some trips.[8] In the 1950s and 1960s, however, technology did not seem to be on the side of the passenger trains, perhaps in part because much of the public funding of transportation research was directed at air and highway transportation.

A very different perspective on the decline of passenger trains holds that differences in public subsidies for various transportation modes caused the decline or at least contributed to it. National, state, and local governments have spent enormous sums in direct net subsidies to road and highway programs and, to a lesser degree, air travel. According to one estimate, those subsidies amounted to approximately $150 billion for highways and $40 billion for air travel between 1920 and 1978.[9]

Perhaps the most striking example of differential subsidies occurred during the Great Depression, when the owners of nearly one-third of the nation's rail mileage were simultaneously filing for bankruptcy.[10] Although the federal government did provide some financial help to railroads during the Depression,[11] that assistance pales in comparison to the treatment given the highway system. At one point during the Depression, net subsidies covered nearly two-thirds of the entire cost of highway programs.[12] If the railroads had received comparable help, they would have been in a much better position to attract and retain passenger traffic.

A number of railroads did receive substantial subsidies, including land grants, cash gifts, and loan guarantees, when much of the nation's rail system was originally built. However, these subsidies were largely repaid through discounts that the recipient firms provided for shipment of government goods and for troop movements.[13] In contrast, there is no serious movement among public policymakers to require comparable repayment of the subsidies given to road or air transportation.

The issue of government support is highlighted also in the controversy over the U.S. Post Office's decision to remove virtually all first-class mail from passenger trains in 1967, the culmination of a process that had been underway on a piecemeal basis for more than a decade. It has been argued that this loss was the final blow to private passenger train service. The post office's decision was followed by a substantial number of requests by railroads to terminate their passenger trains.[14]

Critics of this perspective contend that much of the mail handled by the railroads was bulk mail that generated relatively little revenue relative to its costs. Mail may have been little more than a break-even proposition at best.[15] In addition, most of the decisions to remove mail service from individual trains between 1953 and 1966 were at the request of the railroads.[16] One assumes, therefore that mail service had not been enormously profitable. At any rate, the loss of mail service can hardly be blamed for causing the death of passenger trains in cases when the railroads requested the removal.

Most of the nation's passenger trains were terminated before 1967, the year in which the general policy removing first-class mail from the trains was established. Even if mail service had been somewhat profitable, the gains from it evidently were not nearly enough to offset the losses passenger trains were incurring. In that case, railroads that were trying to eliminate services that were unprofitable overall sensibly might request removal of marginally profitable mail business that could give regulatory authorities a reason to require continuation of that service. One set of statistics does stand out, however, in this context. Annual passenger train losses were quite stable from 1961 through 1966; they ranged from $375 million to $398 million. In 1967, with the loss of mail service, the losses jumped by 21 percent, to over $460 million.[17] No other increase of remotely comparable magnitude exists from 1957 through 1970. Railroad executives would have had to be extraordinarily serene individuals to avoid being alarmed by such an increase, especially against a backdrop of substantial losses for a number of years.

Overall, to the degree that major public subsidies for road and air travel caused the decline of passenger trains, a very different policy response than that suggested by the technology perspective may be in order. Equalizing subsidies may yield a more efficient allocation of transportation resources. The existence of subsidies for other modes, however, does not in itself provide a convincing justification for subsidizing passenger trains. Passenger trains would have to produce benefits that are comparable to the benefits of road and air travel. This issue will be explored more fully in subsequent chapters.

A rather different collection of perspectives places substantial blame for the decline of passenger trains on the railroads. Obsolete work rules limited productivity and made labor costs unnecessarily high. Passenger trains were placed at a significant disadvantage relative to airplanes, buses, and automobiles as a result.[18] Critics complained in the late 1950s of trains that failed to arrive on schedule and of equipment that was often old, dirty, and inadequately heated or cooled. Ticketing and reservation systems were inconvenient, and personnel sometimes were rude. Some of the railroads did little to advertise their services. They seemed to be trying to drive passengers away.[19] In the pungent words of one railroad executive, "We're still listed as running passenger service . . . , but we try not to do it. God damn all passengers on a short haul, anyway. . . . If . . . I have to carry passengers I'll make it so uncomfortable, inconvenient, and disagreeable for them that they'd wish they never bought a two-bit ticket."[20]

The decline of light rail and interurban rail systems further contributed to passenger discouragement. Early in the twentieth century, people who traveled on intercity trains could make easy connections, using light rail and interurban rail systems that provided convenient access to many destinations. Those systems gradually declined, in part as a result of competition from automobiles, governmental decisions that hampered their operations, and competitors who purchased and dismantled some of the systems in order to increase demand for automobiles and buses.[21]

The discouragement hypothesis holds that the railroads themselves decided to discourage people from traveling by rail. One version of this hypothesis asserts that passenger trains were clearly losing money because of technological changes and subsidies for competing modes. Therefore, the railroads were simply trying to minimize their losses in the face of a hopeless situation. The second version contends that passenger trains may have been profitable or at least potentially profitable but that railroad executives could not or would not help them to survive and prosper.[22] At first glance this viewpoint suggests an element of economic irrationality: what sort of entrepreneur abandons a profitable enterprise? However, students of bureaucratic politics may find a plausible explanation for that apparent irrationality.

Part of the explanation is rooted in leadership recruitment. Because the nation's railroads generate most of their incomes from freight operations, top management of most railroads always has been dominated by executives whose background is in freight operations. They are generally knowledgeable about freight operations but less expert in the passenger arena, where success depends more on attention to mass marketing, comfort, and convenience.[23] In addition, rail freight and passenger operations present railroads with somewhat conflicting demands. Passenger trains, with their higher speeds, require higher banking on curves than is optimal for freights. Operating freight and passenger trains on the same track also can cause delays and scheduling problems as operators try to route trains around one another.[24] Given these factors and the background of the decisionmakers, railroad executives might have decided that the best solution to the conflicting demands was the elimination of passenger trains.

Although the innermost thoughts of railroad executives from 1920 to 1970 are largely irretrievable, several observations are possible. First, the bulk of the evidence on passenger train losses indicates that to the degree that the railroads did act to discourage passenger traffic, whether by acts of commission or of omission, they were trying to minimize losses rather than dismantle a profitable operation. Second, the railroads clearly did not take some steps that might have promoted passenger train travel: more aggressive advertising, more convenient ticket and reservation systems, and in the later years of private service, careful maintenance of equipment. To the degree that they were losing money on passenger traffic, of course, they had little incentive to devote resources to a money-losing service.

On the other hand, many of the railroads did make substantial efforts to attract and retain passenger traffic. From 1946 through the mid-1950s, the railroads invested considerable sums in new passenger cars and locomotives. Dome cars, improved sleeping cars, and a host of other new equipment were put into operation to improve the appeal of rail travel.[25] Substantial sums also were spent on rebuilding older equipment to make it more comfortable and attractive. This enormous and costly effort to modernize the passenger rail fleet seems inconsistent with the view that railroad executives saw no value in rail passenger service.[26] In addition, passenger railroad timetables of the late 1950s are filled with a host of efforts to attract the public, including discount fares, descriptions of on-board amenities, low-cost meals, and other attractions. In spite of those efforts, however, ridership continued to decline, and the financial losses continued.

The discouragement hypothesis is significant in that its converse implies that a management team committed to the success of passenger trains could stop their long-term decline and even increase passenger volume. Leaders who understand the particular needs of passenger service, including attractive advertising and customer comfort and convenience, might even make passenger rail service profitable. This hypothesis, however, in accounting for the decline of passenger trains, does not address the technological lead or greater access to subsidies enjoyed by road and air systems, or the relationships among subsidies, technological development, and railroad leadership perspectives.

The Implications of the Decline

The decline of passenger trains elicited a variety of reactions. Many citizens evidently were not interested in the situation, a hardly surprising response in view of the many other events of the late 1950s and 1960s. The plight of passenger trains seemed much less dramatic than the civil rights movement, the Vietnam War, or riots in large cities. Some analysts regarded the decline of passenger trains as the natural result of market forces weeding out the obsolete and unnecessary.[27] Other observers, however, expressed alarm at the prospect of a nation without passenger trains.

Some of their concerns center on the environmental consequences of total reliance on road and air transportation. Both require enormous amounts of land for the roads themselves, airports, parking, and service facilities. By one estimate, the three largest air terminals in the New York City area occupy enough land to provide a double-track railroad right of way from New York City to Chicago.[28] Automobiles and airplanes are also significant sources of air pollution and, especially for airplanes, noise pollution.[29]

A transportation system that is totally dependent on road and air travel also presents congestion and access problems. A number of the nation's main airports are operating at or near capacity, and the same can be said for many highways, at least during peak periods. Moreover, approximately 25 million people are afraid to fly or unable to fly for health reasons, and as many as 40 million cannot drive or do not have access to an automobile.[30] The disappearance of the passenger train would mean the end of an option for dealing with all of those problems.

One other set of concerns regarding the impending disappearance of the passenger train has been rooted in the intersection of transportation and national security, an often neglected connection.[31] During World War II, U.S. railroads demonstrated an impressive ability to move huge quantities of freight and passengers with comparatively limited resources.[32] Of America's major passenger and freight transportation modes, only railroads can, with proven technology, be dependably operated without large quantities of petroleum fuels—most commonly in recent years by electrified rail systems. Relying increasingly on road and air transportation, the United States has committed itself to a nearly total dependence on oil, in huge volumes, for both passenger and freight transportation. The results have not been difficult to predict: declining domestic petroleum reserves, heavy dependence on imported oil, and vulnerability to supply disruptions due to embargoes, sabotage, or military attack.

During the 1960s several forces began to push for national action in response to the decline of passenger trains. Railroad executives grew increasingly unwilling to bear the financial losses caused by passenger trains. Railroad employees grew increasingly concerned about passenger-related jobs. Citizens and officials expressed alarm over the problems that might result from excessive reliance on road and air transportation. The growing financial problems of many northeastern railroads added a further sense of urgency. As a number of studies of policy innovation have found, a crisis often helps to stimulate action on a policy issue.[33] Not surprisingly, however, supporters of action did not have a clear consensus on what sort of action would be most appropriate. Moreover, not everyone agreed on the need to preserve passenger trains.

The National Government Responds

By 1969, specific proposals had surfaced to preserve passenger trains. The board of directors of the Association of American Railroads called for public subsidies for passenger rail service and for a publicly owned pool of passenger equipment. Their proposal offered the railroads help in meeting both operating costs and capital costs. The call for subsidies was echoed by the Interstate Commerce Commission later in 1969. Congressional hearings began on those and a number of other proposals in that same year. Much of that activity took place in the Senate Commerce Committee's Subcommittee on Transportation, chaired then by Senator Vance Hartke.[34]

The Congressional movement to preserve rail passenger service presented the Nixon administration with an awkward problem. An outright subsidy to private firms could lead to a never-ending financial commitment that might escalate enormously over time. Even so, some sort of preservation program seemed likely to pass. The Department of Transportation, led by Secretary John Volpe, responded with an alternative proposal. It called for creating a semipublic corporation, Railpax, which would operate needed passenger trains with a modest infusion of public funding. In the ensuing weeks the administration sent forth remarkably conflicting signals regarding the status of the Railpax proposal. On January 18, 1970, the Department of Transportation announced that the proposal soon would be sent to Congress. On the following day the White House Press Secretary Ron Ziegler said that the White House was not likely to approve submitting the proposal to Congress. Nine days later Secretary Volpe reaffirmed his support for the Railpax proposal and predicted that the White House would approve it within a brief period of time. On the following day, a spokesman for the Bureau of the Budget said that several plans were being considered and that he had no idea which would be approved or when.[35]

In the absence of clear signals from the Nixon administration, Senator Hartke's subcommittee began work on a subsidy bill. This effort was spurred on by the financial problems of the Penn Central Railroad, which operated numerous passenger trains, and by a new round of proposed passenger train terminations. The White House, fearing the cost of a subsidy over the long term, approved informal discussions with Congress on the Railpax proposal, and a revised version was drafted under the leadership of Senators Hartke and Winston Prouty. That proposal, with increased funding, was enacted on October 14, 1970. Another round of administration wrangling followed, with some White House staffers urging a presidential veto and the Department of Transportation and the railroads pressing for presidential approval. President Nixon ultimately signed the legislation, at least in part because it offered the potential for lower costs than a direct subsidy program.[36]

In several respects the Railpax system, later renamed Amtrak, was expected to pursue contradictory objectives, a common phenomenon in policymaking. Supporters wanted it to make a profit but also to maintain nationwide service, thus requiring continuation of unprofitable routes. Some observers expected it to revive passenger train service, but others believed it should serve as a vehicle to eliminate all remaining service and then cease to exist. Some observers called for major investment in new equipment, but others emphasized the need to restrain costs.[37] Nixon administration officials hoped that the quasi-public corporation approach would provide considerable presidential control over the system, but members of Congress believed that the same approach would give Congress considerable leverage. The system's prospects for satisfying all these conflicting expectations were slim indeed.

Early Problems

The Amtrak system began its operations with considerable haste and little chance for advance planning. The legislation that created the system was signed into law on October 30, 1970; its directors were appointed on December 18. Its president was not chosen until April 28, 1971, however, and the system began operations three days later. Although a limited amount of planning was possible, the speed with which the system went into operation meant that numerous problems were unresolved when services began.[38]

A number of the problems were an outgrowth of the condition of the passenger trains in the waning years of private operation. Trying to minimize their financial losses, the railroads had largely stopped investing in new equipment and left obsolete systems in place rather than paying to modernize them. When Amtrak began operations, its average car and locomotive were more than twenty years old, and many were not in very good condition. The climate control systems of many cars had changed little since the days of steam locomotives. Quite a number of cars had features unique to individual railroads and consequently were not readily interchangeable. Moreover, Amtrak inherited thirteen different manual reservation systems, an arrangement that made booking trips difficult and inconvenient.[39]

The financial difficulties of some railroads, particularly in the Northeast, caused additional problems. Several of those railroads had neglected to maintain their track adequately. The combination of poor track and old equipment led to low train speeds and a frequent inability to keep trains on schedule. Many passenger stations also showed signs of years of neglect.[40]

A problem that particularly concerned some observers was Amtrak's unexpectedly rapid depletion of its initial funds. Less than six months after it began operations, it requested a supplemental appropriation. Since Amtrak's original budget request had been developed before many organizational and policy issues had been resolved, a certain degree of difference between projected and actual expenses was to be expected.[41] There can be little doubt, however, that Amtrak's initial appropriation of only $40 million, coupled with just under $66 million income from the railroads in Amtrak's first year, pales in comparison with the private passenger train losses of nearly $450 million in 1970. That initial appropriation was unrealistically low for an effort to create a new organization, upgrade service quality, and operate services that had lost large sums for years.

A related point of contention involved Amtrak's route structure. Amtrak was directed initially to operate at a profit (a goal that was revised later to minimize losses) but also to operate a nationwide system, a requirement that virtually assured continuation of at least some unprofitable routes. As a result, some critics complained that Amtrak was providing service on too many routes with limited traffic, at the same time that other critics complained that the system was too small and served too few routes. The Nixon White House originally favored a very limited number of routes in hopes of restraining costs. However, when Transportation Secretary Volpe, a supporter of passenger rail service, threatened to resign over the issue, the White House accepted a larger initial route structure. Wrangling over routes would continue for eight years, culminating in a significant restructuring in 1979.[42]

A final problem was an outgrowth, at least in part, of uncertainty regarding Amtrak's future. When Amtrak began its operations, the bulk of the actual work still was being done by the railroads that had presided over the decline of passenger trains in the pre-Amtrak era. To a large degree,

Amtrak's performance was in the hands of employees of other railroads. In addition, Amtrak did not own the passenger train stations, terminals, or maintenance facilities that were essential to its operations.[43] Managing for improved performance was hampered by Amtrak's limited control over the personnel and facilities that provided many of the services. Relying on the contracting railroads helped to minimize the seniority complications that might have resulted from shifting large numbers of railroad employees to Amtrak. On the other hand, this reliance reduced the number of people with direct employment interests in Amtrak's survival.

In sum, Amtrak began its operations facing several mutually reinforcing obstacles to its success. First, its equipment was old, and much of it was in poor condition. The prolonged lack of private investment in passenger train equipment meant, furthermore, that virtually no state-of-the-art passenger equipment was available in the United States.[44] Therefore, replacing obsolete locomotives and cars would be difficult.

Moreover, track conditions were poor, particularly in parts of the northeastern United States. Amtrak began operations with no track of its own, and persuading financially troubled railroads who owned the track to improve it for Amtrak's benefit was not an easy task.

In addition, as we have seen, the distribution of Amtrak service generated substantial criticism. The route structure was criticized simultaneously for being too limited, too extensive, and inappropriately distributed. Adding routes risked increasing costs, and terminating service risked angering the public and members of Congress.

Finally, Amtrak faced the daunting task of reversing the long-term decline in passenger train ridership. Many Americans in 1971 had never ridden a passenger train, and many others had not traveled by train for years. Could they be persuaded to begin or return to train travel? If the decline could not be reversed, Amtrak could not hope to justify its existence for long.

The Plan of the Book

The following chapters explore a number of the issues facing the Amtrak system. Chapter 2 provide a descriptive overview of the major changes that have taken place in the system since its creation. Chapter 3 examines the controversy over the distribution of Amtrak service across the country and assesses different explanations for that distribution. Chapter 4 discusses the role of state governments in supporting Amtrak service, investigating why some states have been more supportive than others. Chapter 5 looks at the somewhat volatile international service offered by Amtrak. Chapter 6 addresses the passenger volume handled over the years, and Chapter 7 considers the system's financial performance. Finally, Chapter 8 offers an evaluation of the Amtrak system as a whole.

Notes

1. Patrick Dorin, *Amtrak Trains and Travel* (Seattle: Superior, 1979), 8; Peter Lyon, *To Hell in a Day Coach* (Philadelphia: Lippincott, 1968), 226–227.

2. Dorin, 8; George Hilton, *Amtrak* (Washington, DC: American Enterprise Institute, 1980), 2–4; Lyon, 229; R. Kent Weaver, *The Politics of Industrial Change* (Washington, DC: Brookings, 1985), 42.

3. George Edwards and Ira Sharkansky, *The Policy Predicament* (San Francisco: W.H. Freeman, 1978), 87–88.

4. Don Phillips, "Railpax Rescue," in *Journey to Amtrak,* ed. Harold Edmonson (Milwaukee: Kalmbach, 1972), 8; Hilton, 3–4; John Stover, *The Life and Decline of the American Railroad* (New York: Oxford, 1970), 193; Weaver, 89; Frank Wilner, *The Amtrak Story* (Omaha: Simmons-Boardman, 1994), 24–28.

5. See especially Lyon, 246–248.

6. For analyses of the deficit issue, see "Money Is Roadblock to Revival of Passenger Trains," *Congressional Quarterly Weekly Report,* February 6, 1970, 353; David Morgan, "Who Shot the Passenger Train?" *Trains* 19 (April 1959): 17; James Nelson, *Railroad Transportation and Public Policy* (Washington, DC: Brookings, 1959), 284–314; Stover, 218–221; Weaver, 89, 227.

7. Roger Bradley, *Amtrak* (Poole, United Kingdom: Blandford, 1985), 27; George Drury, *The Historical Guide to North American Railroads* (Milwaukee: Kalmbach, 1985), 12; Hilton, 8; J.B. Hollingsworth and P.B. Whitehouse, *American Railroads* (London: Bison, 1977), 31; Stover, 193; Weaver, 30.

8. See David Nice, "Consideration of High-Speed Rail Service in the United States," *Transportation Research* 23A (1989): 359–365; *U.S. Passenger Rail Technologies* (Washington, DC: Office of Technology Assessment, OTA-STI-222, 1983).

9. Dorin, 11.

10. Drury, 11; Oliver Jensen, *American Heritage History of Railroads in America* (New York: Bonanza, 1975), 289.

11. Lyon, 170.

12. N. Kent Bramlett, *The Evolution of the Highway User Charge Principle* (Washington, DC: Federal Highway Administration, 1982), 23.

13. Dorin, 11–12; George Harmon, *Transportation: The Nation's Lifelines* (Washington, DC: Industrial College of the Armed Forces, 1968), 94; Stover, 228.

14. Drury, 12; "Money Is Roadblock," 354; Stover, 196–197; Karl Zimmerman, *Amtrak at Milepost 10* (Park Forest, IL: PTJ Publishing, 1981), 3.

15. Morgan, 29–31; Nelson, 308–309.

16. Lyon, 250–252.

17. The figures are found in Hilton, 4.

18. See Hilton, 11; Hollingsworth and Whitehouse, 34; Morgan, 20–21; Stover, 197, 200; Wilner, 29.

19. See the criticism in Morgan, 50; Nelson, 321; and especially Lyon, 233–236, 244, 267–268.

20. Quoted in Lucius Beebe, *Mixed Train Daily*, 4th ed. (Berkeley, CA: Howell-North, 1961), 59.

21. See John Due, "The Evolution of Suburban and Radial Rail Passenger Transportation in the United States," Office of Research Working Paper No. 96-0143 (Urbana-Champaign: College of Commerce and Business Administration, University of Illinois, 1996), 24–25; Jensen, 291.

22. See Bradley, 40–41; Lyon.

23. Morgan, 25.

24. Weaver, 227.

25. Edmonson, 5; Jensen, 290; Lyon, 239–240; Stover, 214–217.

26. Stover, 218.

27. See Hilton.

28. Stover, 279.

29. Bradley, 48.

30. Bradley, 48.

31. See *Army Deployment: Better Transportation Planning Is Needed* (Washington, DC: General Accounting Office, 1987); Paul Gardiner, "National Transportation Policy and National Defense: Partners or Apart?" *Proceedings of the Transportation Research Forum* 19 (1978): 12–19; James Van Fleet, *Rail Transport and the Winning of Wars* (Washington, DC: Association of American Railroads, 1956), 4, 59–62.

32. For discussions of these issues, see Wilson Clark and Jake Page, *Energy, Vulnerability, and War* (New York: Norton, 1981); *Energy Security: An Overview of Changes in the World Oil Market* (Washington, DC: General Accounting Office, 1988); David Nice, "Program Survival and Termination: State Subsidies of Amtrak," *Transportation Quarterly* 42 (October 1988): 572–573.

33. Frances Berry and William Berry, "State Lottery Adoptions as Policy Innovations: An Event History Analysis," *American Political Science Review* 84 (1990): 395–416; David Nice, *Policy Innovation in State Government* (Ames: Iowa State University, 1994), 21–25.

34. Phillips, 10; Zimmerman, 6.

35. Phillips, 10; "Money Is Roadblock," 352.

36. Jensen, 299; Phillips, 10–11; Weaver, 88–93.

37. See Bradley, 62; Jensen, 299; "New Railroad Passenger System: Running in the Red," *Congressional Quarterly Weekly Report,* December 18, 1971, 2622, 2624; Weaver, 88–93.

38. See Zimmerman, 2–6.

39. Bradley, 64–68; Dorin, 18; Zimmerman, 3–4.

40. Bradley, 64.

41. "New Railroad Passenger," 2622–2623.

42. See Bradley, 127–135; Mike Shafer, *All Aboard Amtrak* (Piscataway, NJ: Railpace, 1991), 8–9.

43. *Amtrak Sourcebook* (Washington, DC: National Railroad Passenger Corporation, 1988), 5; Weaver, 229.

44. Bradley, 66; Zimmerman, 68.

2

Development: Building the System

Any organization must strike a balance between stability and change, and transportation organizations are no exception.[1] Changing public preferences, new technologies, population movements, and rising or falling prices of supplies may force an organization to make drastic changes in many aspects of its operations. Internal conflicts, employee discontent, and discovery of previously unrecognized performance problems also may stimulate modifications in an organization. All of these forces have been at work in the transportation industry in recent decades.

Although transportation organizations must change at times to keep pace with shifting external conditions and to manage internal pressures, a degree of organizational stability is essential. For example, transportation systems require substantial public and private investment in fixed facilities, vehicles, and personnel training. A high degree of instability risks rendering those investments irrelevant or wasteful.

Amtrak has faced considerable difficulties in trying to achieve the desired balance of stability and change needed to maintain credibility as a transportation mode. Beginning with uncertain and conflicting goals, the Amtrak system seemed to be destined for chaos rather than predictability. Repeated attacks by the Reagan administration, conservatives in Congress, and bus companies seemed to foretell large cutbacks or even termination. Moreover, the nation's passenger train system was in relatively poor condition at the time of Amtrak's creation; maintaining the conditions that existed in 1971 would hardly give the system credibility.

Nonetheless, the Amtrak system has managed to achieve a substantial degree of stability, coupled with significant change—much of it in the nature of improvement. The political turmoil surrounding Amtrak stands in stark contrast to the substantial operational consistency and improvement that the system has achieved.

The Reach of the System

One of the fundamental features of any transportation system is its overall reach: the extent of its routes, the number of access points available on those routes, and the utilization of the routes. A system that experiences rapid expansion of its overall reach is likely to be faced with challenges. Quick expansion brings demands for additional equipment and personnel, as well as the problem of attracting customers in areas not accustomed to service in the past. Rapid contractions bring problems as well: surplus equipment must be stored or disposed of, employees must be reassigned or terminated, and customers facing the loss of service may be upset.

The broad reach of the Amtrak system—as indicated by the route miles covered by the system, the number of stations served, and the number of train miles operated—has displayed significant consistency over time, although some notable variation exists as well (see Table 2.1). The system expanded gradually until the 1979 cutbacks, which included termination of the National Limited, linking New York and Kansas City; direct Chicago–Miami service on the Floridian; the Lone Star, running from Chicago to Texas; and the North Coast Hiawatha, serving Chicago and the Pacific Northwest. Although the cutbacks were not as large as proposed initially,[2] they produced discernible decreases in system route miles, train miles, and stations served—the largest decreases in the system's history.

The 1979 cutbacks did not put an end to the political controversy surrounding Amtrak, but further dramatic cuts in route mileage and train mileage did not follow. Instead, both stabilized quickly and remained approximately at 1980 levels until 1988, when a modest upward trend in train miles began. The 1990s saw Amtrak generating the greatest number of train miles annually in its history. The number of stations served, however, continued to decline after the cutbacks until 1983, when a rough plateau was reached. In the late 1980s, the number of stations served gradually began to increase to roughly the peak levels of the late 1970s.

The system, then, displayed rapid stabilization after the cutbacks of 1979. The number of stations served fluctuated somewhat (within a rather narrow range), but there is a trade-off at play here: maintaining additional access points may attract more customers up to a point, but a greater number of station stops leads to lower train speeds. Ending service to stations that draw very few riders improves travel times and thus actually may increase ridership, particularly among people traveling longer distances.

The costs of additional stations are somewhat variable. For example, one station may offer baggage checking, handicapped access, ticket sales, and baggage storage facilities; every train on the route may stop there. In contrast, another station may serve as a flag stop (trains do not stop there unless a passenger will board or detrain there) with no baggage service and

Table 2.1   The Reach of the Amtrak System

	System Route Miles (in millions)	Stations Served	Train Miles (in thousands)
1972	23	440	26
1973	22	451	27
1974	24	473	29
1975	26	484	30
1976	26	512	31
1977	26	524	33
1978	26	543	32
1979	27	571	32
1980	24	525	29
1981	24	525	31
1982	23	506	29
1983	24	497	29
1984	24	510	29
1985	24	503	30
1986	24	491	29
1987	24	487	30
1988	24	498	30
1989	24	504	31
1990	24	516	33
1991	25	523	34
1992	25	524	34
1993	25	535	35
1994	25	540	34

Source: Annual Report (Washington, DC: National Railroad Passenger Corporation, various issues).

no ticket sales. It may be simply a platform or small waiting room, in which case the cost of serving that station will be modest. The somewhat adjustable costs of serving a station may contribute to a degree of instability in the number of stations served. Stations with minimal services can be added to assess public demand; where demand is insufficient, stations subsequently can be terminated.

The aggregate stability of system reach, as indicated by Table 2.1, should not be overstated. Overall stability may conceal changes that may be quite significant in individual regions. A comparison of Amtrak's 1973 reach with that of 1987 shows great similarity at the aggregate level but some noteworthy changes in particular areas. The 1987 route structure lacked the North Coast Hiawatha, Lone Star, Floridian, and National Limited. However, the 1987 system added direct service from Salt Lake City to both Portland, Oregon, and Los Angeles; service between Chicago and Texas on the Eagle; and New York–Chicago service via Buffalo on the Lake Shore Limited. In addition to altering the availability of rail service, the route modifications have changed significantly the time required for rail travel on some corridors.[3]

The Amtrak Fleet

As noted in Chapter 1, one major aspect of the decline of private passenger service after World War II was the general lack of investment in new equipment, particularly after the mid-1950s. Purchases of new cars and locomotives were postponed or avoided altogether, and modernization of existing equipment was kept to an absolute minimum on most railroads. Consequently, Amtrak began its operations with a fleet of cars and locomotives that was quite old and obsolete technologically. Equipment problems plagued many trains, and modernization was a critical need for the system.[4]
Amtrak's management devised a multipronged strategy for dealing with its aged car fleet. The worst of the existing cars were retired from service as quickly as possible. Work began on designs for new cars as well, a task made more difficult technologically by the general absence of investment and improvement in passenger rail cars in the 1960s. There also was a significant political issue: ordering new cars implied a commitment that the system was going to continue for quite some time rather than serve as a vehicle for eliminating rail passenger service.

The first new passenger cars were not ordered until 1973 and were not delivered until 1975. These Amfleet cars were designed primarily for short and intermediate trips but are used now in all types of service in the East. Superliner equipment for conditions in the western states required a more dramatic departure from existing designs and thus more funds and time for development. The first Superliner equipment, consequently, was not ordered until 1975 and began service in 1979. Amtrak also embarked on a major program of rebuilding older equipment to modernize its electrical and climate control systems.

The purchase of new cars and the retirement of older ones led to a dramatic but temporary reduction in the average age of Amtrak's car fleet. The reduction subsequently was offset by federal constraints on Amtrak funding, which led to a substantial increase in the age of the passenger car fleet (see Table 2.2). The average car had declined to 13 years old in 1981 and 1984, a nearly 50 percent reduction from the 25-year-old cars typical in 1975, the oldest cars in a quarter century. With funding constraints beginning in the early 1980s, partly because of complaints about the national government's chronic budget deficits, new car purchases were curtailed, and the average age of the fleet began to rise. Amtrak did continue development of new car designs, most notably the Viewliners.[5] These are the first generation of cars designed expressly for long-distance service on eastern trains since Amtrak's creation. Superliner equipment is limited largely to western trains because it is too large for many eastern tunnels and bridges. Amtrak also has tested imported equipment designed to permit higher train speeds on curving track.

The size of the Amtrak car fleet has fluctuated considerably over the years. The fleet expanded noticeably through 1976 and then began a

Table 2.2   The Passenger Car Fleet

	Revenue Cars	Average Age (years)
1972	1,569	22
1973	1,717	23
1974	1,881	24
1975	1,882	25
1976.	1,932	20
1977	1,806	20
1978	1,678	20
1979	1,607	20
1980	1,589	14
1981	1,436	13
1982	1,450	14
1983	1,480	15
1984	1,379	13
1985	1,523	14
1986	1,664	15
1987	1,705	16
1988	1,710	17
1989	1,742	18
1990	1,863	20
1991	1,786	21
1992	1,796	22
1993	1,853	23
1994	1,852	22

Source: Annual Report, various issues,

decline that presaged the 1979 train terminations. Fleet size hit bottom in 1984, but a rebuilding program resulted in a substantial rebound. The Heritage Fleet of rebuilt cars has been the mainstay of long-distance trains in the eastern portion of the country and includes coaches, sleeping cars, diners, and lounge cars.

A rail system's speed and reliability are heavily dependent on its motive power. Of course, track conditions and coordination with other traffic are crucial as well, but a passenger rail system cannot function effectively without fast and dependable locomotives. Amtrak began its operations with a fleet of old and obsolete locomotives that hampered efficient operations. As with passenger cars, few passenger locomotives were purchased in the waning years of private passenger train service; as a result, the development of passenger locomotives lagged considerably. The system's early efforts to develop new passenger locomotives were not terribly successful, but eventually it settled on the F40 and AEM-7, both of which proved themselves in extensive service. These two models formed the backbone of Amtrak's locomotive fleet for a number of years, with the AEM-7 on electrified routes and the F40 on other corridors. As the F40s reached the end of their useful operating lives in the 1990s, Amtrak began to acquire more advanced diesels from General Electric. These new locomotives, some of which are rated at 4,000 to 4,200 horsepower, eventually will handle all trains on nonelectrified routes.[6]

Amtrak's average locomotive was more than a generation old when the system began operations, but the replacement program reduced the average age to only four years by 1981 (see Table 2.3). As is the case for passenger cars, the budgetary constraints since 1981 have curtailed locomotive purchases greatly, although matters improved somewhat during the mid-1990s. With fewer locomotives being purchased, the average age of the fleet tripled between 1982 and 1990.

The locomotive modernization program and the financial constraints since 1981 have had major consequences for the average availability of the locomotive fleet. Old locomotives require more maintenance and heavy repair work; they are more prone to mechanical breakdowns. In Amtrak's early years, locomotive availability fluctuated considerably, with one-fourth of the fleet being out of service on a typical day in 1979. As new locomotives came into service and older units were retired—note that the total size of the locomotive fleet declined by nearly 60 units between 1979 and 1983—the proportion of units unavailable for service on a typical day

Table 2.3   The Locomotive Fleet

	Average Age (years)	New Deliveries	% Out of Service[a]	Locomotives
1972	22	0	NA[b]	185
1973	19	40	NA[b]	337
1974	14	110	24	442
1975	14	30	13	362
1976	11	51	17	353
1977	10	0	20	330
1978	7	10	19	320
1979	7	10	25	331
1980	7	12	17	301
1981	4	75	14	295
1982	4	18	12	278
1983	5	10	11	273
1984	6	0	8	284
1985	7	10	7	291
1986	8	0	8	291
1987	9	0	11	289
1988	10	10	13	298
1989	11	13	16	312
1990	12	0	16	318
1991	13	0	14	316
1992	13	20	17	329
1993	13	26	16	334
1994	13	18	15	338

Source: Annual Report, various issues.
[a]Daily average.
[b]Not available.

declined to well below 10 percent in the early 1980s. However, with the budgetary constraints of the 1980s and consequent limitations on new locomotive purchases, the rising age of the locomotive fleet helped to spur a substantial increase in the proportion of the fleet unavailable for service on a typical day: the proportion of locomotive units out of service on an average day rose from 7 percent in 1985 to 17 percent in 1992. The aging of the locomotive fleet has been the subject of considerable criticism from some observers and is part of a broader pattern of aging U.S. infrastructure, including roads, water systems, bridges, and airports.[7]

One other development regarding the locomotive fleet deserves mention. Amtrak's newer locomotives are significantly more powerful than its first-generation equipment. As a result, each locomotive can handle more traffic than was the case in the early years. For example, in 1973, each locomotive hauled an average of 11.3 million passenger miles of traffic annually. By 1994, the average locomotive hauled an average of 17.5 million passenger miles of traffic.

On-Time Performance

Modernization of equipment has many goals, including increased passenger comfort and safety, a more positive public image, and lower maintenance costs. However, one of the most important reasons for modernizing equipment lies in increasing dependability. A system that cannot deliver passengers as scheduled risks driving away customers and losing public support. Moreover, if people cannot obtain reliable information regarding travel times because a transportation system fails to meet its schedule, they cannot make fully rational transportation decisions. An individual who chooses a particular transportation mode in the belief that it is faster than a competitor will have made a poor choice if the chosen mode is actually slower than the competition. Travelers may miss their connections with other transportation modes if arrivals are late.

In Amtrak's early years it had considerable difficulty meeting schedules, particularly on long-distance trains (see Table 2.4). Although arrival times are affected by many factors, much of Amtrak's early difficulty resulted from the age and condition of its equipment. As new cars and locomotives came into service, on-time performance improved steadily from 1979 through 1983. Once again, however, the rising age of equipment beginning in the early 1980s was reflected in a slump in on-time performance after 1983. The decline was most notable on long-distance trains. Diesel locomotives, which are used on virtually all long-distance trains, have comparatively shorter operating lives; electric locomotives, which pull the short-distance trains between New Haven and Washington, DC, normally have longer operating lives and are less affected by an incremental

Table 2.4   On-Time Performance of Amtrak Trains

	Systemwide	Short Distance	Long Distance
1972	75%	82%	53%
1973	60	70	30
1974	75	80	63
1975	77	80	72
1976	73	75	67
1977	62	66	48
1978	62	65	52
1979	57	61	48
1980	69	71	64
1981	77	77	76
1982	79	79	81
1983	82	81	82
1984	80	81	77
1985	81	82	78
1986	74	76	69
1987	74	78	62
1988	71	76	54
1989	75	81	54
1990	76	82	53
1991	77	82	59
1992	77	82	61
1993	72	79	47
1994	72	78	49

Source: Annual Report, various issues.

increase in age. The Northeast Corridor Improvement Project, with its substantial investment in track repair and development, also has helped improve on-time performance on the many short-distance trains in the northeast. It is noteworthy that Amtrak owns the Northeast Corridor, where its fastest trains operate. Most of its routes in the rest of the country are on tracks owned by freight railroads; their sensitivity to the scheduling needs of their own freight movements increases the risk of passenger train delays.

Passenger Volume

Amtrak was created after a prolonged period of declining ridership on passenger trains, and some observers doubted that there was any realistic hope of bringing back the customers. Amtrak's survival, however, required attracting considerable numbers of new train passengers for at least two reasons. First, it needed customers to generate revenues. Although the proportion of Amtrak's funds derived from customers has varied over the years, customer revenues always have been a substantial portion of the system's total income, a point to be examined in more detail shortly. Second, without customers the system cannot maintain the political support that is essential to its existence. Satisfied customers may convey their satisfaction to elected officials. In contrast, a train that attracts very few customers is obviously unlikely to appear valuable to many public officials.

Predictable, reliable growth in ridership, however, has been problematic in the period since Amtrak's creation. Fluctuations in the price and availability of gasoline have at times altered the appeal of traveling by car. Airline deregulation has yielded changes in airfares, sometimes on a daily basis, as well as increases in air service on some corridors and decreases on others. The economy has ranged from serious recession to prosperity, with substantial variation from one region of the country to another. The Amtrak system has added new routes and abandoned others, added new equipment, and created a nationwide ticketing and reservation system. It has faced and defeated proposals for its termination. Overall, the political, economic, and transportation environment generally has presented a number of obstacles to sustained growth in Amtrak ridership.

Trends in Amtrak ridership can be examined in Table 2.5. The number of passengers carried in intercity service surged in 1974 during the energy crisis, declined in 1975, then rebounded, reaching a plateau of roughly 21 million passengers annually from 1979 through 1981. The recession of the early 1980s is reflected in a decline in ridership, followed by another rebound that, with some hesitations, eventually reached a plateau of approximately 22 million riders annually in the 1990s, the highest level in the system's history. By 1986, Amtrak was carrying more passengers than Republic Airlines, Continental, or TWA in scheduled domestic service.[8] Note, too, that the passenger volume in Table 2.5 includes intercity passengers only. In 1987, Amtrak began operating commuter trains for the Massachusetts Bay Transportation Authority. Its operations there and in Maryland carried over 10 million passengers in 1987, and commuter traffic rose to 33 million passengers in six states by 1994, bringing total volume to 55 million passengers.[9]

Trends in passenger mileage show considerable similarity to trends in the number of passengers carried, but with a significant difference. Passenger miles rose with the energy crisis of the early 1970s, slumped in 1975, then rose until 1979, when the 1979 service reductions and subsequent recession produced a decline in passenger miles through 1982, although the decline was not as consistent as that displayed by the number of passengers carried. As with passengers carried, passenger miles began a rebound in 1982. Passenger miles rose each year from 1982 through 1991, to a level more than double the passenger mileage generated in 1972. A modest slump followed, with passenger mileage hovering around the 6 billion mark in the 1990s.

The tendency for passenger miles to rise proportionally faster than the number of passengers carried reflects an increase in the length of the average trip after 1985. Improved travel times on some corridors and a

Table 2.5   Amtrak Passenger Volume (in millions, intercity traffic only)

	Passengers	Passenger Miles
1972	17	3,038
1973	17	3,806
1974	19	4,258
1975	17	3,939
1976	19	4,221
1977	19	4,333
1978	19	4,029
1979	21	4,915
1980	21	4,582
1981	21	4,762
1982	19	4,172
1983	19	4,246
1984	20	4,552
1985	21	4,825
1986	20	5,013
1987	20	5,221
1988	22	5,678
1989	21	5,859
1990	22	6,057
1991	22	6,273
1992	21	6,091
1993	22	6,199
1994	22	5,921

Source: Annual Report, various issues.

national advertising campaign may have helped to spur more long-distance travel, a trend that may be reinforced by the addition of various amenities, including movies, on long-distance trains. Additional equipment may be needed, however, to accommodate further increases in long-distance traffic volume during peak travel periods.[10]

Financing the System

Supporters and critics alike have followed closely the financial performance of the Amtrak system. Although all transportation modes in the United States receive subsidies, Amtrak's subsidies have been unusually controversial. In part this may reflect the comparatively recent nature of passenger train subsidies, in contrast to long-established subsidies for road and water transportation and air travel. In addition, some subsidies for other transportation modes are scattered among national, state, and local budgets, and some do not appear in any budget. For example, income tax deductions help finance automobile purchases (by permitting deduction of interest costs, whether directly or through home equity loans) and thus constitute a subsidy that is comparatively concealed.

A full historical perspective is essential for assessing the current subsidy situation. The Amtrak system was created after an extended period of disinvestment in passenger trains. Locomotives and cars were not replaced or upgraded on many lines, as private railroads tried to minimize passenger train losses in the late 1950s and 1960s. No integrated, nationwide system for passenger train ticketing and reservations existed. The technology for creating such a system was available, but the railroads, struggling with passenger train deficits running into hundreds of millions of dollars, had little incentive to expand access to a money-losing service.

If the United States essentially stopped investing in road transportation for a period of ten to fifteen years—virtually no new roads built, no new cars or trucks purchased, existing roads not expanded or upgraded— a decision to revive road transportation would yield years of costs much higher than those required if the system had been following a consistent program of maintenance and upgrading each year. A period of disproportionately high costs is inevitable in any system that must compensate for past decisions to postpone investments.

The financial performance of the Amtrak system clearly reflects the legacy of the past as well as the existence of subsidies to other transportation modes. Operating expenses have exceeded revenues substantially, particularly during the late 1970s and early 1980s, when investments in new equipment were at a high level (see Table 2.6). However, the financial picture shows some quite positive aspects. Operating revenues have increased almost every year, exceeding $1.4 billion in 1993 and 1994. Expenses have risen as well, but the growth rate for expenses has been substantially more modest than revenue growth since the late 1970s. From 1980 through 1994, operating revenues grew by approximately 229 percent, while expenses grew by only 126 percent. As a result, the ratio of operating revenues to expenses grew from .39 in 1980 to .80 in 1993, the highest level achieved in Amtrak's history, then declined slightly to .77 in 1994. To some degree the improvement appears to be related to the slowdown in equipment purchases (a point that will be explored later), but a sensitivity to holding down costs and improving the revenue picture is valuable for any transportation system.

Financial improvements have resulted from a number of factors in addition to the slowdown in equipment purchases. Rising passenger miles have contributed to a firm revenue base, but other operations also have boosted Amtrak's income. Mail and express revenues reached $60 million in 1994, and real estate transactions added another $38 million. New labor agreements have enhanced productivity and helped restrain growth in costs.[11] The use of one-person locomotive crews in the Northeast Corridor saves an estimated $16.5 million annually, compared with two-person crews, according to an analysis by the General Accounting Office.[12] Taken together, the financial improvements led to a major milestone in 1987:

Table 2.6 Amtrak's Financial Performance

	Operating Revenue (in millions)	Operating Expenses (in millions)	Revenues/ Expenses
1972	$162	$286	.57
1973	202	345	.59
1974	257	498	.52
1975	253	567	.45
1976	278	666	.42
1977	311	784	.40
1978	313	842	.37
1979	381	952	.40
1980	429	1,103	.39
1981	496	1,252	.40
1982	558	1,186	.47
1983	664	1,469	.54
1984	659	1,522	.56
1985	826	1,600	.58
1986	861	1,564	.62
1987	974	1,672	.65
1988	1,107	1,757	.69
1989	1,269	1,935	.72
1990	1,308	2,012	.72
1991	1,359	2,081	.79
1992	1,325	2,037	.79
1993	1,403	2,134	.80
1994	1,413	2,490	.77

Source: Annual Report, various issues.

Note: Changed accounting methods in 1978 may affect comparisons between 1977 and earlier with later years.

Amtrak's revenues produced by intercity train operations exceeded short-term avoidable costs for the first time in its history. By the early 1990s, Amtrak officials began to envision an era when Amtrak's earned revenues would cover all of its operating costs.[13] However, in all likelihood Amtrak would continue for the foreseeable future to need financial assistance to cover the cost of capital equipment.

Toward the Future

The development of the Amtrak system in the past provides clues to future developmental needs. According to some observers, the overall reach of the system could be expanded prudently by establishing rail service between large cities that are reasonably close to one another—probably no more than three hundred miles apart—along corridors that are densely populated.[14] These corridors offer the potential of adding significant traffic volume while requiring only modest additions to the aggregate system.

Modest expansion can be achieved at modest cost and reduces the risk of overbuilding and of escalating expectations beyond the system's capacity to satisfy them on a sustained basis.

The Amtrak car fleet is hard pressed to handle reliably the system's traffic volume, especially during peak periods. While production and delivery of the new Viewliner cars will be helpful for modernization of the eastern fleet,[15] the Heritage Fleet, the mainstay of long-distance eastern trains, continues to age. In a related vein, the aging of the locomotive fleet is grounds for serious concern. A sustained program of locomotive replacement, buttressed by constant attention to maintenance and, when needed and feasible, rebuilding, is essential to system performance. Unreliable locomotives lead to late trains, missed connections, and unhappy customers. Relying on excessively old locomotives results in high maintenance costs and decreased availability as aging equipment requires more and more maintenance to keep operating.[16] Although new locomotives have been acquired during the mid-1990s, the replacement process has been slower than desirable for assuring reliable performance.

The Amtrak system needs to establish and maintain a long-term capital investment program to provide adequate system capacity and to permit continuous modernization of equipment as needed. That program in turn will require a comparatively stable and adequate level of funding from the national government, rather than the considerable fluctuations in capital funding that have occurred over the years. In constant 1995 dollars, Amtrak's capital funding from the federal government has varied from more than one billion dollars annually to only $20 million in fiscal year 1986.[17] Whether the White House and Congress will deviate from their previous pattern of boom and bust is highly uncertain.

Because rail travel is most economical with high traffic volume, Amtrak would do well to continue its efforts to increase ridership as part of its efforts to improve financial performance. Its management must be alert constantly to potential threats and opportunities resulting from the external transportation environment. In the face of competing modes, the growth in passenger miles since Amtrak's formation indicates that its efforts to build traffic volume have been relatively successful. Nationwide and local advertising, discount fares, and the Travel Planner, with its combination of information about routes, accommodations, hotel and tour packages, and attractive illustrations, are all likely to be part of continuing marketing efforts. Improvements in on-board amenities, including movies, games, and telephone service, also have demonstrated their value in enhancing the appeal of train travel.[18] The experience of the Los Angeles–San Diego corridor attests to the value of state and local government participation; on that corridor, track improvements, more frequent service, and attractive stations—all made possible by state and local government support—along with coordinated transportation connections, spurred a dramatic increase in ridership.[19] A leadership team committed to attracting passengers has demonstrated that it can be done.

In sum, Amtrak's financial performance shows signs of significant improvement. Further improvements are still needed. On the revenue side, expanding passenger volume can help to increase revenues, a point that will be explored more closely in a later chapter. In addition, the revenue potential of nonpassenger operations deserves additional effort. Funds received from mail and express service, from contract work (including assembly and rebuilding work for other railroads), and from real estate transactions are likely to continue to be important for the foreseeable future; a financially hard-pressed organization must seek revenues wherever they can be found. At the same time, continuing efforts to control costs are essential. Productivity improvements are important in all public organizations, and Amtrak is no exception.

Notes

1. For discussions of the virtues of stability and change, see Ira Sharkansky, *The Routines of Politics* (New York: Van Nostrand Reinhold, 1970); Everett Rogers, *Diffusion of Innovations,* 3rd ed. (New York: Free Press, 1983).

2. See Rodger Bradley, *Amtrak* (Poole, United Kingdom: Blandford, 1985), 126–127, 135; Karl Zimmerman, *Amtrak at Milepost 10* (Park Forest, IL: PTJ Publishing, 1981), 74.

3. David Nice, "Changing Program Performance: The Case of Amtrak," *Transportation Journal* 27 (1987): 44–45. For an overview of route changes, see Mike Schafer, "Amtrak's Atlas," *Trains* 51 (June 1991): 49–53.

4. Bradley, 73–75; Frederick Stephenson, *Transportation USA* (Reading, MA: Addison-Wesley, 1987), 173–175; Frank Wilner, *The Amtrak Story* (Omaha: Simmons-Boardman, 1994), chapter 4.

5. Tom Nelligan, "The Viewliner Venture," *Passenger Train Journal* 19 (March 1988): 16–22.

6. Bradley, 66–73, 142–148; Wilner, 73–74.

7. See "News Photos," *Passenger Train Journal* 18 (May 1987): 7; Simon Webley, *Stiffening the Sinews of the Nations* (London: British–North American Committee, 1985); Pat Choate and Susan Walter, *America in Ruins* (Durham, NC: Duke, 1981).

8. *Annual Report* (Washington, DC: National Railroad Passenger Corporation, 1986), 11.

9. *Annual Report* (Washington, DC: National Railroad Passenger Corporation, 1987), 1–3; *Statistical Appendix to Amtrak FY 1994 Annual Report* (Washington, DC: National Railroad Passenger Corporation, 1994); Wilner, 94.

10. *Annual Report*, 1987, 3; "The Journal," *Passenger Train Journal* 19 (June 1988): 4.

11. *Annual Report*, 1987, 6–7, 9; *Statistical Appendix*.

12. *Amtrak's Northeast Corridor Trains Operate with a One-Person Locomotive Crew* (Washington, DC: General Accounting Office, 1985), iii–iv, 13–14, 20.

13. *Annual Report*, 1987, 3; *Annual Report* (Washington, DC: National Railroad Passenger Corporation, 1993), 2.

14. See *National Transportation Trends and Choices* (Washington, DC: Department of Transportation, 1977), 193; see also *Annual Report* (Washington, DC: National Railroad Passenger Corporation, 1994), 7.

15. *Annual Report*, 1987, 3; "Journal Update," *Passenger Train Journal* 22 (May 1991): 13.

16. For a step in that direction, see *Annual Report*, 1987, 5; *Annual Report*, 1994, 13–14.

17. *Annual Report*, 1994, 13.

18. The services and amenities vary from train to train. The *Amtrak National Train Timetables* (Washington, DC: National Railroad Passenger Corporation, periodic) contain information on amenities for each train.

19. See Carl Schiermeyer and L. Erik Lange, "The Making of a Corridor," *Passenger Train Journal* 19 (February 1988): 16–21.

3

Distribution:
Who Gets Service?

As noted earlier, the distribution of Amtrak service has been a subject of controversy at a number of points in its history. When the system was first established, critics decried the absence of service on some routes; that criticism led to the addition of several trains. Additions and cutbacks in service have been proposed and adopted on several occasions, with mixed results.[1] The early Amtrak system offered direct service between Chicago and Florida and between New York and St. Louis that is not available today (although connections can be made with a change of trains). Conversely, direct service between Chicago and Buffalo was not part of the original system but is available now. Wyoming had passenger rail service under the original Amtrak system, then lost it for several years, regained it, and now lost it again.

The amount of service provided by Amtrak varies greatly from state to state. New York, with approximately 10 percent more rail mileage than Oklahoma, has more than three hundred trains weekly while Oklahoma has no service at all. Wyoming and Mississippi have approximately equal rail mileage, but Mississippi has considerably more Amtrak service than does Wyoming. In view of the variation in service from one part of the country to another, the availability and distribution of services has been a continuing issue.

A number of studies have sought to explain variations in the geographical distribution of public programs and benefits generally. In some instances, the distribution of benefits and services reflects, at least in part, the exercise of political influence on behalf of local concerns. Individual neighborhoods, communities, or regions may mobilize to gain benefits for themselves based on how much political power they have rather than any defensible standard of need or merit. Political considerations may shape the timing of announcements of benefits and the speed with which claims are processed and may also influence service and benefit levels.[2] Public officials sometimes complain that their home states or districts are being

31

shortchanged in the distribution of public services, which suggests that political careers may be affected by that distribution.[3]

Program needs, often defined in terms of relatively impersonal decision rules, also affect the distribution of public services. Distribution may be shaped by professional norms or by bureaucratic decision rules made in response to particular aspects of a problem environment.[4] This chapter will seek to explain variations in the distribution of Amtrak service across the United States by drawing on studies of both local and national service distributions. The resulting findings may help to cast light on how national policymakers allocate program benefits across the country, a task that must be done for many programs. Before examining the data, a number of hypotheses will be explored that bear on decisions regarding distribution of services.

Influences on the Distribution of Amtrak Service: Bureaucratic Decision Rules

Many studies of the distribution of public services and on intergovernmental grants emphasize the role of bureaucratic decision rules in defining the problem environment and establishing responses to it.[5] General decision rules for allocating services may follow several premises.[6] Efficiency criteria seek to allocate services to provide the most benefits for the lowest cost.[7] In contrast, service may be allocated in accordance with demand, usage, or potential revenue contributions; areas where recreational programs are poorly attended, for example, may experience reductions in program offerings, while areas with heavy attendance may gain programs. A compensatory strategy, however, tries to use service distributions to offset or overcome disadvantages, as in the case of a school system that gives additional resources to schools with large numbers of students from poor families.

Transportation research suggests a basic cost consideration underlying several efficiency criteria. Transportation analysts generally contend that rail transportation has relatively high fixed costs.[8] Consequently, passenger rail service is likely to be most efficient where traffic volume is high. A number of strategies for achieving high traffic volume exist.

First, a geographically concentrated population is likely to provide greater traffic volume for a given investment in facilities. A widely dispersed rural population would require a very extensive passenger rail system, much of which would carry relatively little traffic.[9] The prospects for cost-effective service would be slim. A denser, more metropolitan population can be connected with fewer routes and, consequently, is more likely to produce the traffic volume needed to justify the high fixed costs of passenger rail service.

In addition to population density, absolute numbers may shape service as well. A large population is more likely to produce high traffic volume than is a small one, other things being equal. A state with several million residents can generate considerable passenger volume even if only a small proportion of the population travels by rail. A state with only a few hundred thousand residents, in contrast, is unlikely to generate much volume unless residents have an unusually high propensity to travel by train.[10]

One other component of the task environment with efficiency implications is distance. Trains cannot match the speed of airplanes when in motion, but train stations typically are closer to downtown than are airports. Consequently, rail travel times may be roughly comparable to travel time by air over short-to-intermediate distances if the time needed to travel to and from terminals is taken into account.[11] States in which population centers are comparatively close to population centers in other states will be particularly suitable for passenger train service, according to this criterion.

A final efficiency-related criterion, as reported in a U.S. Department of Transportation study, is the combination of a large population *and* geographical proximity.[12] A large population creates a large potential customer pool, but rail travel is most likely to tap that pool if the distances traveled are short enough to produce competitive travel times. According to this hypothesis, states that combine large populations and comparative closeness to population centers in other states are more likely to provide an environment conducive to efficient passenger train operations. Overall, efficiency criteria should lead to more extensive service in more metropolitan, densely populated states with population centers that are close to major population centers in adjacent states.

A compensatory strategy presents a very different framework for allocating services. Amtrak has sometimes been presented as a mechanism for providing mobility for people who are too poor to own a car or fly.[13] The compensatory strategy suggests that services should be concentrated in poorer states, where proportionally more people would be in need of mobility assistance.

A demand-oriented strategy would present the opposite tendency. Because Amtrak derives a substantial share of its revenues from its customers,[14] and because it has been under considerable fiscal pressure over the years, it might be inclined to provide disproportionately high levels of service to areas wealthy enough to generate large numbers of paying customers.[15] A pattern of unusually high service levels in wealthier states also would be consistent with the underclass hypothesis, which contends that class biases in the political system lead poorer areas to receive less than their fair share of public services, other things being equal.[16]

Political Forces

Although bureaucratic decision rules may shape the way a public agency distributes its services, political considerations also may play a role. A widely recognized strategy of public agencies seeking to survive and prosper is the cultivation of political clienteles, who receive program benefits in exchange for providing political support.[17] Given that much of the battle over Amtrak's survival has taken place in Congress, route distribution may in part be linked to relationships between legislators and their constituents.[18] Moreover, impressionistic evidence suggests that the need for political support sometimes has influenced the distribution of Amtrak service.[19]

One political force that might affect the distribution of service is interparty competition. In a competitive political environment, votes are valuable. Consequently, members of Congress may feel greater pressure to support programs that may earn the gratitude of voters, even when those programs are out of favor with party leaders.[20] Where officeholders face little threat from the opposition party, conversely, they may feel less pressure to deliver benefits to constituents. A public agency seeking to build or maintain support, therefore, is likely to benefit from providing additional services to politically competitive areas.

A second political consideration that also may shape the distribution of service is ideology. Generally speaking, liberals are more supportive of government intervention in the economy, whereas conservatives prefer a limited governmental role.[21] Moreover, congressional voting often follows ideological lines.[22] Although substantial governmental involvement in the transportation field has a long history in the United States, conservatives have often criticized Amtrak, particularly during the Reagan administration.

If Amtrak uses services to mobilize support, the ideological climate may shape that effort in at least two ways. First, if Amtrak uses a strategy of building a solid but limited base of support, it is likely to provide more services to liberal areas with liberal congressional delegations. In effect, this strategy uses service and ideology to reinforce one another: ideological liberalism, which encourages Amtrak support, is buttressed by service benefits. This strategy risks creating an intense opposition coalition of members who are hostile on ideological grounds (that is, conservative) and whose districts receive few or no benefits. Conversely, if Amtrak has a strategy of maintaining a broad base of support, even if it is not a particularly solid base, then service may be used to offset ideological forces. In this strategy, more conservative areas would receive more service, in hopes that they would support the system, while liberal areas would receive less service but would be expected to provide support on ideological grounds.[23] These same choices based on ideology might also apply to distribution of services according to Republican or Democratic dominance in given areas, with decisions based on the premise that Republicans have been more hostile generally to Amtrak. The supposition here, of course, is that much congressional decisionmaking is played out, at least partially, along party lines.[24]

For administrators involved with established programs, however, allocation of services based on partisan or ideological criteria carries substantial risks over the long term. If some partisan or ideological groups feel short-changed in the distribution of program benefits, a subsequent increase in the size of those groups in the legislature may leave the program with many opponents. Consequently, administrators of ongoing programs may prefer to avoid partisan or ideological allocation strategies in order to minimize the program's vulnerability to political shifts.[25]

Likewise, some legislators occupy positions on subcommittees that handle agency authorizations or appropriations, and those members' support is particularly crucial to agency survival and growth.[26] An agency that seeks to use services to mobilize support could be expected to provide additional service to areas represented on the subcommittees that have particular influence on the agency. However, a representative's re-election is not always assured, and, furthermore, not all congressional committees are equally committed to producing district benefits.[27] Moreover, members of Congress tend to gravitate to committees with control over programs that are important to the members' districts.[28] Overall, factors directly related to legislative politics are only one set of influences on service distributions.

Another potential influence on the distribution of Amtrak service is state subsidies.[29] The legislation creating Amtrak provided that states can obtain additional service by helping to pay for that service, and a number of states have adopted subsidies at one time or another. State subsidies might reflect bureaucratic decision rules, political considerations, or both (a topic we will examine in some detail later), and they may shape service distributions across the country. The state-subsidized trains, however, comprise a quite small fraction of the national system.

The structure of the nation's rail system also affects distribution of Amtrak service. Although Amtrak service has improved as a result of track rehabilitation work on some routes, funding never has been sufficient either to construct new railroad lines or to maintain or significantly upgrade very many of them. However, all the continental forty-eight states have significant rail mileage, and most of the variation in the distribution of service from state to state involves the frequency of service on a few routes rather than the number of different routes served.

Data and Methods

The distribution of Amtrak service is measured by the number of trains per week (one way) serving each state. The variation is considerable, from states that have more than three hundred trains weekly to states that have no Amtrak service at all. Information on service levels is taken from the *Amtrak National Train Timetables*.[30]

Data on metropolitanization is from the *Statistical Abstract*.[31] Population, population density, and per capita income figures are from the *World Almanac*.[32] Geographical isolation is measured in two ways. First, the mean distance from the state capital to the three nearest state capitals was calculated. Second, the mean distance was calculated from the largest city in the state to the three nearest cities, each of which is the largest city in its respective state. Distance figures are derived from the *Rand McNally Road Atlas*.[33]

Interparty competition is measured by the Ranney index[34] and the Bibby, Cotter, Gibson, and Huckshorn index.[35] Both indices are based on gubernatorial and legislative election results and are folded so that high scores indicate high levels of party competition. Previous research indicates that state political currents quite readily spill over into congressional politics.[36]

Electoral ideology is measured in two ways. First, the percentage of the two-party vote for George McGovern in the 1972 presidential election, which had strong ideological overtones,[37] gives a relatively behavioral indication of ideological leanings. Second, an estimate of the electorate's ideological self-identification based on pooled public opinion surveys[38] gives a more direct assessment of the opinion climate. Both measures are related to a variety of state policy decisions.[39] The ideological leanings of state congressional delegations is measured by the mean Conservative Coalition support score for each state delegation,[40] in addition to the mean of the state delegation means for both chambers. In a similar fashion, the percentage of Democrats in each state delegation for each chamber was calculated, along with the mean of the two chamber percentages.

Four subcommittees are particularly relevant for Amtrak: the Senate Appropriations Committee's Subcommittee on Transportation and Commerce, the Senate Science and Transportation Committee's Subcommittee on Surface Transportation, the House Appropriations Committee's Subcommittee on Transportation and Public Works, and the House Transportation Committee's Subcommittee on Surface Transportation. States were given one point for each member of the delegation on any of these four subcommittees.[41]

Data on state subsidies are taken from *Amtrak: Cost of Amtrak Railroad Operations*.[42] States were coded one if they subsidized Amtrak service for at least two-thirds of the year and zero otherwise.

Analysis

The zero-order relationships between the distribution of Amtrak service by state, on one hand, and a number of indicators of the relative efficiency of passenger rail service are consistent with virtually all of the initial hypotheses (see Table 3.1). States with more extensive Amtrak service tend to be more metropolitan, densely populated, and populous. In addition, service is more extensive in states that have capitals and largest cities that

Table 3.1   Needs, Suitability, and Amtrak Service

| | Amtrak Trains per Week[a] | |
	All States	Alaska/Hawaii Excluded
Percentage metropolitan, 1980	.61**	.63**
Population density, 1980	.66**	.66**
Population density (square root)	.73**	.74**
Population, 1980	.53**	.52**
Population (square root)	.55**	.53**
Capital distance	−.35**	−.45**
Capital distance (square root)	−.46**	−.49**
Large city distance	−.21	−.07
Large city distance (square root)	−.36**	−.28*
Population divided by capital distance[b]	.75**	.74**
Population divided by large city distance[b]	.79**	.77**
Per capita income, 1982	.31*	.49**

[a]Square root transformation to correct for skewness. Derived from *Amtrak National Train Timetables,* April 28, 1985.

[b]Square root transformation of quotient.

*Significant at the .05 level. Coefficients are Pearson's r.

**Significant at the .001 level. While the use of significance tests with a population is controversial, they are included here to give an indication of the likelihood that the relationships could be due to chance. See Hubert Blalock, *Social Statistics,* rev. 2nd ed. (New York: McGraw-Hill, 1979), 241–243.

are relatively close to their counterparts in nearby states. Finally, states that have proportionally large populations relative to the physical isolation of their capitals and largest cities—that is, states with large populations and capitals or largest cities close to their counterparts in nearby states— have more extensive Amtrak service.

The contrasting expectations of the demand and compensatory approaches are resolved in favor of the former, at least at the zero-order level. States with more extensive Amtrak service tend to be more affluent, although the relationship is not as strong as the relationships produced by most of the efficiency-based measures.

The analysis indicates that excluding Alaska and Hawaii usually has little impact on the relationships, but some exceptions do exist. The relationships between service, on one hand, and per capita income and capital distance are stronger when Alaska and Hawaii are omitted (passenger rail service in Alaska is provided by the Alaska Railroad, which is state owned). In contrast, the relationships for large city distances are somewhat weaker when Alaska and Hawaii are omitted. Note, too, that Amtrak service is more strongly related to several state traits when those traits are measured using a square-root transformation. The differences typically are small, although the increase for large city distance is substantial. Overall, the zero-order findings are consistent with the perspective that the distribution of service reflects efficiency criteria to a substantial degree and, to a lesser degree, affluence.

The zero-order relationships between the distribution of Amtrak service and political characteristics also tend to be consistent with most of the political hypotheses, although the relationships tend to be weaker than those produced by efficiency and demand characteristics. Amtrak service tends to be more extensive in politically competitive states as measured by Ranney, but not according to the more recent Bibby, Cotter, Gibson, and Huckshorn index. Political liberalism is associated with more extensive service, whether liberalism is assessed at the electoral level or at the level of congressional delegations (see Table 3.2).

The partisan composition of state congressional delegations fares somewhat unevenly in explaining Amtrak service distributions. States with more heavily Democratic House delegations tend to have more extensive Amtrak service, as expected, but the partisan composition of U.S. Senate delegations essentially is unrelated to service levels. Averaging the House and Senate proportions does not improve the predictive power of partisan composition. In contrast, committee representation is related strongly to Amtrak service distributions; states with more members of Congress on Amtrak-relevant subcommittees do tend to have more extensive service. However, given the tendency for members to gravitate to committees that control programs of interest to their constituents,[43] the distribution of Amtrak service may influence members' preferences for subcommittee assignments rather than the subcommittee positions influencing services.

Finally, states that subsidize Amtrak service tend to have more extensive service, as expected. Interpretation of this relationship at the zero-order level is difficult, however. State subsidy decisions may reflect efficiency concerns as well as other political considerations.[44]

Because of the large number of independent variables, stepwise regression analysis[45] was used to develop a parsimonious model of the bureaucratic decision rules that influence the distribution of Amtrak service (see Table 3.3). The results indicate that Amtrak service tends to be more extensive in states that have large populations relative to the distances from the largest city in the state to the three nearest cities, each of which is the largest city in its respective state. In other words, a populous state with its largest population center located relatively closely to the major population centers in adjacent states tends to have more extensive service. In addition, more densely populated states tend to have more extensive service.

The preliminary bureaucratic model indicates that, broadly speaking, states in which passenger rail service is most efficient tend to have the most passenger rail service. A large, concentrated population geographically close to major population centers in adjacent states is more likely to produce travel times that are competitive with alternative transportation

Table 3.2   Political Characteristics and Amtrak Service

	Amtrak Trains per Week[a]	
	All States	Alaska/Hawaii Excluded
Party competition (Bibby, et al., 1983)	.05	.07
Party competition (Ranney, 1976)	.26*	.27*
Percentage for McGovern, 1972	.32*	.34**
Electoral conservatism	−.56***	−.56***
Conservative Coalition support, Senate	−.40***	−.44***
Conservative Coalition support, House	−.39***	−.41***
Conservative Coalition support, joint	−.43***	−.46***
Percentage Democratic, Senate	.08	.09
Percentage Democratic, House	.24*	.26*
Percentage Democratic, joint[b]	.19	.21
Subcommittee representation	.44***	.44***
Subcommittee representation (square root)	.34***	.33***
State subsidy	.46***	.45***

[a]Square root transformation.
[b]Mean of Senate and House values.
*Significant at the .05 level.
**Significant at the .01 level.
***Significant at the .005 level.

Table 3.3   Regression Analysis of Amtrak Service Distribution: Needs and Appropriateness Model[a]

	b	beta	t
Population divided by large city distance[b]	2.40	.51	4.62***
Population density[a]	.26	.40	3.68***
a = −.47			−.66
R² = .69			

[a]Square root transformation. Alaska and Hawaii excluded.
[b]Square root transformation of quotient.
***Significant at the .001 level. All predictors in Table 3.1 were eligible for inclusion in the model.

modes and is also likely to produce high traffic volume, which is needed in view of the high fixed costs of passenger rail service. Overall, the bureaucratic model accounts for more than two-thirds of the variation in service from state to state.

Preliminary multivariate analysis of the political influences on the distribution of Amtrak service produces somewhat ambiguous findings (see Table 3.4). Service tends to be more extensive in states with a more liberal climate of opinion, as expected, and in states that subsidize Amtrak service. Both findings are ambiguous, however, because state subsidies may reflect efficiency concerns as well as political influence, as noted earlier, and because a more metropolitan population may create simultaneously more acceptance of government activism[46] and an environment in which passenger rail service is more efficient.

An initial test of the first ambiguity can be performed by deleting state subsidies from the predictor list and re-estimating the model. When that is done, electoral conservatism emerges as the only significant predictor of the distribution of Amtrak service, and the predictive power of the model drops by roughly one-fourth (see Table 3.4). A more definitive assessment of those ambiguities requires a model that incorporates both bureaucratic decision rules and political influences.

An integrated model of the distribution of Amtrak service indicates that efficiency criteria play a substantial role and that political factors exert modest but significant influence (see Table 3.5). As in Table 3.3, states with large populations relative to the distance to major population centers in adjacent states tend to have more extensive Amtrak service, as do more densely populated states. In addition, however, service tends to be more extensive in politically competitive states, as predicted by the marginality hypothesis. The improvement in explanatory power relative to the bureaucratic model is comparatively modest, but the improvement constitutes a reduction in the unexplained variance (of the bureaucratic model) of just over 11 percent. None of the other variables examined in this analysis could significantly improve the fit of the model.

The relationships between the distribution of Amtrak service, on one hand, and the two efficiency indicators (population relative to distances from major population centers in adjacent states and population density) are able to survive the addition of controls for the variables that do not appear in the final model when they are introduced one at a time. However, the relationship between service and interparty competition is sensitive to the inclusion of other controls, particularly those that tap ideological tendencies in the mass public or state congressional delegations. Nonetheless, since those variables cannot survive controls for the bureaucratic variables, while the bureaucratic variables in Table 3.5 can survive controls for the political variables, the choice of the final model is relatively straightforward.

Conclusions

Public controversies over government programs sometimes leave the casual observer with the impression that the flow of benefits is largely a function of the ability to twist arms, make large campaign contributions, or persuade elected officials. People who mobilize political influence of one kind or another will gain from governmental activities, while people who lack political influence will receive little or nothing, in this view. To the

Table 3.4   Regression Analysis of Political Influence on Amtrak Service Distribution[a]

	b	beta	t
General political model[b]			
Electoral conservatism	−.28	−.48	−4.16**
State subsidy	4.30	.35	3.05*
a = 9.10			7.55**
R^2 = .43			
Restricted political model[c]			
Electoral conservatism	−.33	−.56	−4.53**
a = 10.97			8.62**
R^2 = .31			

[a]Square root transformation. Alaska and Hawaii excluded.
[b]All predictors from Table 3.2 were eligible for inclusion in the model.
[c]All variables from Table 3.2 except state subsidy were eligible for inclusion in the model.
*Significant at the .005 level.
**Significant at the .001 level.

Table 3.5   Regression Analysis of Amtrak Service Distribution: Full Model[a]

	b	beta	t
Population divided by large city distance[b]	2.33	.49	4.70**
Population density[a]	.26	.40	3.79**
Party competition (Ranney, 1976)	.07	.19	2.36*
a = −2.62			−2.30*
R^2 = .72			

[a]Square root transformation. Alaska and Hawaii excluded.
[b]Square root transformation of quotient.
*Significant at the .05 level.
**Significant at the .001 level. All predictors from Tables 3.1 and 3.2 were eligible for inclusion in the model.

degree that the constellation of political forces fails to reflect the problem environment, the flow of public benefits may bear little resemblance to efficiency concerns or the distribution of needs.

As numerous observers have noted, however, the drama of election campaigns, public speeches, and decisions by elected officials does not lead to precise control over the operation of public programs.[47] Administrators often find that guidance from the public and its elected representatives is relatively vague and leaves the bureaucracy with significant discretion in allocating resources. One result of this phenomenon is that the distribution of public benefits may reflect the nature of the problem environment, at least as it is defined by bureaucratic decision rules.

Moreover, elected officials are not preoccupied entirely with maximizing localized benefits in order to build political support or with pursuing a set ideological agenda. Many officials are concerned to a significant degree with developing practical, workable solutions to policy problems.[48]

Therefore, they may press for policies that include efficiency concerns, compensatory provisions, and/or demand considerations. Bureaucratic decision rules do not emerge from a vacuum; they may reflect interactions among administrators, elected officials, and a variety of other actors.[49]

The continuing battle over the future of Amtrak naturally has led people in that agency to be concerned with maintaining and building political support.[50] The need for political support apparently has shaped some Amtrak service decisions in the past.[51] Those considerations might well be appropriate for explaining variations in the distribution of Amtrak service.

The preceding analysis indicates that a perspective oriented toward bureaucratic decision rule has considerable merit in explaining Amtrak service availability. Efficiency criteria derived from the transportation literature are quite effective in accounting for the distribution of service. Once the characteristics of the task environment, as indicated by those criteria, are taken into account, political considerations involving nonefficiency criteria play a modest but significant role.

It is true that program variations that appear small from a national perspective may seem substantial from the perspective of an individual state or community. Moreover, the political variables examined here do not include information on members' personal goals or interests. Overall, however, most of the variation in Amtrak service across the country can be explained by long-established indicators of efficiency.

Notes

1. George Hilton, *Amtrak* (Washington, DC: American Enterprise Institute, 1980), 15–20; Roger Bradley, *Amtrak* (Poole, United Kingdom: Blandford Press, 1985), 123–135.

2. Theodore Anagnoson, "Federal Grant Agencies and Congressional Election Campaigns," *American Journal of Political Science* 26 (1982): 547–561; Frederic Bolotin and David Cingranelli, "Equity and Urban Policy: The Underclass Hypothesis Revisited," *Journal of Politics* 45 (1983): 217–218; Martha Derthick, *Uncontrollable Spending for Social Services Grants* (Washington, DC: Brookings, 1974); Bryan Jones, "Party and Bureaucracy: The Influence of Intermediary Groups on Urban Public Service Delivery," *American Political Science Review* 75 (1981): 688–700; David Koehler and Margaret Wrightson, "Inequality in the Delivery of Urban Services: A Reconsideration of Chicago Parks," *Journal of Politics* 49 (1987): 95.

3. R. Douglas Arnold, *Congress and the Bureaucracy* (New Haven: Yale, 1979), 3; Robert Dilger, "Grantsmanship, Formulamanship, and Other Allocational Principles," *Journal of Urban Affairs* 5 (1983): 269–286; John Ferejohn, *Pork Barrel Politics* (Stanford: Stanford University, 1974), 49–50.

4. See Arnold, 20; Robert Lineberry, *Equality and Urban Policy* (Beverly Hills: Sage, 1977), 153–156; Kenneth Mladenka, "The Urban Bureaucracy and the Chicago Political Machine: Who Gets What and the Limits to Political Control," *American Political Science Review* 74 (1980): 991–998.

5. See Bolotin and Cingranelli, 218–219; John Boyle and David Jacobs, "The Intracity Distribution of Services: A Multivariate Analysis," *American Political Science Review* 76 (1982): 376–377; Lineberry, 153–157.

6. Arnold, 20, 44–46; Boyle and Jacobs; Koehler and Wrightson.

7. Efficiency concerns are a recurrent theme in Amtrak's *Annual Report* (Washington, DC: National Railroad Passenger Corporation). See the 1986 issue, 3–4, 7–9; 1987, 3, 9, 11; 1993, 2–5; 1994, 2, 7–14. The following analysis will focus on efficiency concerns in a relatively narrow sense and will not address some broader efficiency issues, such as the national security aspects of a rail passenger system and the long-term energy situation. That decision is based in part on the heavy emphasis that narrow efficiency concerns have received in the debate over Amtrak. In addition, the implications of some of the broader efficiency concerns for Amtrak's route structure are not very clear at this point. We will explore some of those broader issues in Chapter 8.

8. Donald Harper, *Transportation in America*, 2nd ed. (Englewood Cliffs, NJ: Prentice-Hall, 1982), 222.

9. A similar tendency exists for highways. See Thomas Dye, *Politics in States and Communities*, 4th ed. (Englewood Cliffs, NJ: Prentice-Hall, 1981), 430–431.

10. For evidence of population's influence on state subsidies of Amtrak, see Chapter 4.

11. Hilton, 67.

12. *National Transportation Trends and Choices* (Washington, DC: U.S. Department of Transportation, 1977), 193.

13. For a discussion and critique of that position, see *Federal Subsidies for Rail Passenger Service: An Assessment of Amtrak* (Washington, DC: Congressional Budget Office, 1982), 20–21.

14. *Annual Report* (1986), 3.

15. For assessments of the affluence of Amtrak customers, see *Federal Subsidies*, 20–21.

16. See Lineberry, 57–60.

17. Francis Rourke, *Bureaucracy, Politics, and Public Policy*, 3rd ed. (Boston: Little, Brown, 1984), 52.

18. Ferejohn, 49–50; Aaron Wildavsky, *The Politics of the Budgetary Process*, 2nd ed. (Boston: Little, Brown, 1974), 66–67.

19. R. Kent Weaver, *The Politics of Industrial Change* (Washington, DC: Brookings, 1985), 229–237; Karl Zimmerman, *Amtrak at Milepost 10* (Park Forest, IL: PTJ Publishing, 1981), 25, 74.

20. On the influence of electoral marginality, see Morris Fiorina, "Electoral Margins, Constituency Influence, and Policy Moderation: A Critical Assessment," *American Politics Quarterly* 1 (1973): 479–498; Barbara Sinclair Deckard, "Electoral Marginality and Party Loyalty in House Roll Call Voting," *American Journal of Political Science* 20 (1976): 469–481; however, see also Richard Fenno, *Home Style* (Boston: Little, Brown, 1978), 10–18, 233–234.

21. Lyman Sargent, *Contemporary Political Ideologies*, 5th ed. (Homewood, IL: Dorsey, 1981), 65–68.

22. William Shaffer, *Party and Ideology in the United States Congress* (Lanham, MD: University Press of America, 1980).

23. On coalitional strategies, see Arnold, 44–45; Rick Wilson, "An Empirical Test of Preferences for the Political Pork Barrel: District Level Appropriations for River and Harbor Legislation, 1889–1913," *American Journal of Political Science* 30 (1986): 729–754.

24. Roger Davidson and Walter Oleszek, *Congress and Its Members*, 2nd ed. (Washington, DC: CQ Press, 1985), 388–391.

25. Arnold, 53, 68.

26. On the importance of subcommittees, see Steven Smith and Christopher Deering, *Committees in Congress* (Washington, DC: CQ Press, 1984), chapter 5.

27. Richard Fenno, *Congressmen in Committees* (Boston: Little, Brown, 1973).

28. Nicholas Masters, "House Committee Assignments," *American Political Science Review* 55 (1961): 345–357.

29. David Nice, "The States and Amtrak," *Transportation Quarterly* 40 (1986): 559–570.

30. (Washington, DC: National Railroad Passenger Corporation, April 28, 1985). There are other possible measures of service, including the range of on-board services available and travel times. However, the on-board services are largely standardized on long-distance trains (sleeping accommodations on overnight runs, food service, and the like) and among shorter-distance trains as well, with some minor exceptions. Travel times are heavily influenced by track conditions, which are primarily the responsibility of the private railroads that own most of the track on which Amtrak operates. Amtrak's fastest trains operate on its own track, the bulk of which is in states with the most trains per day.

31. (Washington, DC: Bureau of the Census, 1982), 16.

32. (New York: Newspaper Enterprise Association, 1983), 116–198.

33. (Chicago: Rand McNally, 1985).

34. Austin Ranney, "Parties in State Politics," in *Politics in the American States,* 3rd ed., ed. Herbert Jacob and Kenneth Vines (Boston: Little, Brown, 1976), 61.

35. John Bibby, Cornelius Cotter, James Gibson, and Robert Huckshorn, "Parties in State Politics," in *Politics in the American States*, 4th ed., ed. Virginia Gray, Herbert Jacob, and Kenneth Vines (Boston: Little, Brown, 1983), 66.

36. Jeffrey Cohen and David Nice, "Changing Party Loyalty of State Delegations to the U.S. House of Representatives, 1953–1976," *Western Political Quarterly* 36 (1983): 312–325; Warren Kostroski, "Party and Incumbency in Postwar Senate Elections: Trends, Patterns, and Models," *American Political Science Review* 67 (1973): 1213–1234.

37. Norman Nie, Sidney Verba, and John Petrocik, *The Changing American Voter* (Cambridge: Harvard, 1976).

38. Gerald Wright, Robert Erikson, and John McIver, "Measuring State Partisanship and Ideology with Survey Data," *Journal of Politics* 47 (1985): 469–489.

39. David Nice, *Policy Innovation in State Government* (Ames: Iowa State University, 1994); Gerald Wright, Robert Erikson, and John McIver, "Public Opinion and Policy Liberalism in the American States," *American Journal of Political Science* 31 (1987): 980–1001.

40. *Congressional Quarterly Weekly Report,* January 11, 1986, 78–80.

41. Charles Brownson, *Congressional Staff Directory* (Mount Vernon, VA: Congressional Staff Directory, 1985).

42. (Washington, DC: General Accounting Office, 1986), 2.

43. Masters.

44. David Nice, "The States and Amtrak"; David Nice, "Program Survival and Termination: State Subsidies of Amtrak," *Transportation Quarterly* 42 (1988): 571–585.

45. For discussions of the advantages and disadvantages of stepwise techniques, see N. R. Draper and H. Smith, *Applied Regression Analysis*, 2nd ed. (New

York: Wiley, 1981), 307–311; Ronald Wonnacott and Thomas Wonnacott, *Econometrics*, 2nd ed. (New York: Wiley, 1979), 407–410.

46. Charles Adrian, *State and Local Governments*, 4th ed. (New York: McGraw Hill, 1976), 42–43; Charles Adrian and Charles Press, *Governing Urban America*, 5th ed. (New York: McGraw-Hill, 1977), 26–27.

47. Michael Lipsky, *Street Level Bureaucracy* (New York: Russell Sage, 1980); Theodore Lowi, *The End of Liberalism*, 2nd ed. (New York: Norton, 1979).

48. On the diversity of officials' goals, see Fenno, *Congressmen in Committees*, chapter 1.

49. For valuable overviews of those interactions, see Arnold; Randall Ripley and Grace Franklin, *Congress, the Bureaucracy, and Public Policy*, 3rd ed. (Homewood, IL: Dorsey, 1984), chapters 2, 3, 8; Koehler and Wrightson, 84–85.

50. Weaver, 237, 247, 254.

51. Weaver, 229–237; Zimmerman, 25.

4

The States:
Reluctant Partners?

For many years transportation policy has been one of the most important responsibilities of U.S. state governments. Transportation programs consistently are one of the four largest items in state budgets, and transportation issues often are major concerns in state elections, the state legislature, and the executive branch.[1]

Although state transportation programs have emphasized roads and highways for most of this century, the states also have a long history of participation in railroading. During the 1800s, when many states lacked rail service, they adopted subsidy programs to encourage expansion of the railroads. Further state involvement in railroading came in the late 1800s when pricing abuses and corruption practiced by a number of railroads led to state regulations. More recently, the wave of bankruptcies and abandonments that has swept the rail industry has brought about new state efforts to preserve rail service. States have tried tax relief programs, loans, subsidies, and even public ownership in an effort to provide rail service that otherwise would be lost.[2]

When the Amtrak system was created, the states were given an additional opportunity to participate in transportation policymaking. The law creating Amtrak provided that states could obtain additional rail passenger service if officials in those states were willing to help pay the costs of the additional service. This provision reflected a recognition of the fact that transportation policies have localized effects as well as national consequences.[3] Services that might not seem necessary from a national standpoint might be very important to a particular state or group of states. Therefore, the states could help to mold the system to meet their individual needs. The provision also reflected the controversies over Amtrak's route structure and concerns about the cost of the system. States where people felt short-changed by the national network could add to it but only if they helped defray the added costs. The next section of this chapter will seek to explain why some states have adopted subsidies while others have not; the following sections will try to explain why some of the subsidy programs have survived while others have been terminated.

State Adoption of Amtrak Subsidies

Research on public policymaking has identified a number of factors that may influence policy decisions. First, the social and economic environment affects many policy decisions. Second, political forces influence many policies. Third, the problem environment (sometimes called the task environment) shapes a variety of public policies. All three factors will be examined here.

A large body of policy research emphasizes the role of social and economic forces in affecting public policies.[4] One of the most important of those forces is affluence; prosperity permits state officials to try things that would be impractical in a poor state. If available resources are strained to meet current responsibilities, state officials may be reluctant to assume additional commitments.[5] According to this perspective, wealthier states should be more likely to subsidize Amtrak service, a comparatively new transportation program.

Evidence regarding the influence of state wealth on subsidy adoptions indicates that wealthier states are in fact somewhat more likely to adopt subsidies but that the tendency is neither very strong nor very consistent (see Table 4.1)—perhaps because none of the state subsidies is particularly large. In 1985, for example, the largest state subsidy of Amtrak was less than $4 million; in 1996, three states spent less than $200,000 on their

Table 4.1   Amtrak Subsidies, 1980: Zero-Order Correlations

	Amount of Amtrak Subsidy[a]	Amtrak Subsidy per Capita
Per capita income, 1979	.39**	.36*
Percentage metropolitan, 1978	.36*	.30*
Tourism spending, 1979	.58**	.37**
Percentage for McGovern, 1972	.37**	.37**
Electoral conservatism[b]	−.33*	−.27
Walker innovation score	.53**	.44**
Savage innovation score	.33*	.32*
Environmental concern[c]	.35*	.28
State population, 1980	.70**	.50**
State land area	.14	.09

[a]Square root transformation.

[b]Gerald Wright, Robert Erikson, and John McIver, "Measuring State Partisanship and Ideology with Survey Data," *Journal of Politics* 47 (1985): 478–480. Scores are unweighted, and the corrected value for Nevada is used.

[c]High environmental concern states (coded 1) ranked in the top 15 in air or water quality control expenditures, 1970–1971. Other states coded 0. *Source:* Charles Jones, "Regulating the Environment," in *Politics in the American States,* 3rd ed., ed. Herbert Jacob and Kenneth Vines (Boston: Little, Brown, 1976), 410–411.

*Significant at the .05 level. Coefficients are Pearson's r.

**Significant at the .01 level.

subsidy programs.[6] In an era of multibillion dollar state budgets, even less affluent states may be able to afford modest subsidies of rail passenger service.

A second important aspect of the socioeconomic environment (although also part of the problem environment for transportation policies) is metropolitanization. The impersonality and interdependence of the metropolis, where many people are affected by one another's actions and where many interactions take place among strangers, are likely to produce more demands for governmental action of many kinds.[7] Furthermore, metropolitanism captures a significant aspect of the problem environment when transportation policies are concerned. Rural states tend to be more oriented to highway building and to spend more on road and highway programs.[8] As a result, fewer dollars are likely to remain for nonhighway transportation programs. In addition, rail transportation has relatively high fixed costs. Unit costs of service will, therefore, be lower with higher traffic volume,[9] a situation most likely to be found in states with relatively concentrated populations. This suggests that rail passenger service is most economical in relatively metropolitan states. To the degree that state officials try to allocate resources productively and in response to public demands, metropolitan states should be more likely to subsidize Amtrak service.

Analysis of state subsidies indicates that metropolitan states are indeed more likely to adopt subsidies and that the tendency is fairly consistent over time.[10] As with affluence, however, the tendency is not a very strong one.

A third aspect of the socioeconomic environment (again, partly an aspect of the problem environment as well) is tourism. Although a substantial number of Amtrak's customers are business travelers, particularly in the Northeast Corridor, many riders are traveling for recreational purposes. Given that many people prefer not to fly and that others dislike driving or are unable to drive,[11] train travel is a potentially important element of the tourist transportation system. States with large tourism industries may have a strong incentive to subsidize Amtrak as a means of maintaining tourist access.

Evidence strongly supports this expectation. States with relatively high levels of spending by tourists are indeed more likely to subsidize Amtrak service, and the relationship tends to be stronger than for either affluence or metropolitanization.[12] In addition to promoting visits from people who cannot or prefer not to fly or drive, passenger rail service may be a form of insurance against future fuel shortages or price increases as far as the state's tourism industry is concerned.

State subsidy decisions may also be influenced by the political environment. Although transportation policies in the United States have not tended to generate the displays of ideological conflict that occur periodically for welfare or tax policies, ideological forces are at work for many transportation decisions. Where political values emphasize individualism and the virtues of private-sector decisionmaking, government intervention in what are viewed as market decisions is likely to be discouraged. Political liberalism, by contrast, provides a more supportive environment for governmental activism.[13]

Analysis of state adoptions of Amtrak subsidies indicates that politically liberal states are somewhat more likely to adopt subsidies but that the relationship is not very consistent. The subsidizing states in 1980 were noticeably more liberal than the nonsubsidizers, but the difference was rather faint in 1985.[14]

A second political factor that may influence adoption of subsidies is innovativeness. While states have been involved with the railroads in various ways since the 1800s, subsidizing Amtrak is a fairly new activity. Research on state policymaking has established that the states vary considerably in the speed with which they adopt new policies.[15] Some states have ample experience with adoption of new programs, and being a pioneer may even be a matter of pride. Elsewhere, traditional practices may be more highly prized. Analysis of adoption of state Amtrak subsidies confirms that innovative states (that is, states with a history of being relatively quick to adopt new programs) indeed are more likely to adopt subsidies and that the tendency is reasonably consistent over time.[16] Where a proposal must struggle against the combined opposition of groups that are hostile to the specific proposal and groups that are suspicious of policy changes in general, the odds of adoption are likely to be low.

One other political factor that may influence state subsidy decisions is concern for the environment. It has long been recognized that transportation policies have significant environmental consequences. Rail transportation can move a given number of people in a smaller expanse of land than can automobiles. Trains consume less fuel per passenger mile than airplanes or, apparently, automobiles. Greater fuel economy results in less pollution as well.[17] To the degree that passenger trains offer environmental benefits relative to other transportation modes, states with comparatively high concern for protecting the environment should be more likely to support passenger rail service. Analysis supports this expectation. States with a record of strong efforts to protect the environment are considerably more likely to subsidize Amtrak service than are other states. Moreover, the pattern is relatively consistent over time.[18]

An additional group of potential influences on subsidy decisions is the problem environment. Many students of public policymaking note that policy decisions often are a reaction to a problem rather than political beliefs or other considerations.[19] In this view, the key to explaining policy decisions lies in the nature of the problems faced by the political system.

As we saw in the discussion of route distribution in Chapter 3, cost-effective rail systems tend to be linked with higher populations. A larger population, therefore, may increase the likelihood that a state will subsidize Amtrak service. In fact, subsidizing states do tend to have large populations. The tendency is among the strongest in Table 4.1 and is fairly stable over time.[20]

Physical size might also be thought to influence subsidy decisions, since larger states might be more inclined to help overcome the barriers created by distance. Analysis indicates, however, that land area is essentially unrelated to Amtrak subsidies. Whether a state is physically large or small tells us little about its decision to subsidize or not subsidize passenger rail service.

Multivariate Analysis of Subsidy Adoptions

Because of the large number of variables of potential interest and the fact that the number of states actually subsidizing Amtrak is relatively small in any given year, stepwise regression analysis was used to generate a relatively parsimonious model of state subsidy decisions.[21] Analysis of 1980 subsidies indicates that state population is a powerful influence on state subsidy decisions and that political liberalism, as measured by the vote for McGovern in 1972, is a moderately important influence as well (see Table 4.2). As we have seen, a large population is more likely to generate the traffic volume needed to make passenger rail service appropriate economically. It also permits a broader distribution of program costs and is more likely to provide a significant pool of program beneficiaries. Not surprisingly, then, the more populous states are more likely to adopt subsidies.

Ideological liberalism, with its broader view of public responsibilities and greater willingness to intervene in the economy, provides a more supportive environment for Amtrak subsidies. However, ideology's influence is substantially smaller than the influence of population. In addition, the

Table 4.2   Regression Analysis of Amtrak Subsidies, 1980

	b	Standard error	beta	Significance
Amount of Amtrak subsidy[a]				
State population[b]	.053	.008	.66	.0000
Percentage for McGovern	.135	.056	.25	.02
	Constant = −5.80	R^2 = .55		
Amtrak subsidy per capita[c]				
State population	.0038	.001	.45	.0007
Percentage for McGovern	.017	.007	.29	.024
	Constant = −.63	R^2 = .33		

[a]Subsidy in tens of thousands of dollars. Square root transformation.
[b]In hundreds of thousands.
[c]Subsidy in tens of thousands of dollars per 100,000 people.

influence of ideological factors in multivariate analysis varies over time; in 1985, subsidizing states were no more liberal than nonsubsidizing states, other things being equal.[22] One sign of that shift was the presence of southern states, which tend to be more conservative, in the ranks of the 1985 subsidizers.

Survival and Termination of the State Subsidies

Government programs sometimes seem to be immortal. Once public agencies are created, they are rarely abolished. Commitments of public funds quickly become entrenched, and groups that benefit from those financial commitments typically resist efforts to reduce or eliminate them.[23] In recent years, however, a combination of rising costs, slow revenue growth, and taxpayer resistance to tax increases has led to reductions in funding for some public programs and, less commonly, to outright terminations of programs.[24] State subsidies of Amtrak service have not been immune to those pressures. A total of fourteen states subsidized Amtrak service for at least part of the period from 1979 through 1986, but by the end of that period eight of them had terminated their subsidies.[25] The following section will seek to determine why some subsidy programs have survived while others have been terminated.

One possible explanation for whether state funding survives centers on the choice of routes that are subsidized. If a state embarks on a subsidy program involving costs that greatly exceed the benefits produced, that subsidy will be vulnerable to public criticism and/or official elimination. If a state chooses a particularly inappropriate route for subsidy, that subsidy may face a greater risk of termination.

Comparisons of routes raise two significant complications. First, some of the states that have subsidized Amtrak service continuously from 1979 through 1986 have changed the routes subsidized. As a result, the following analysis will emphasize the routes that have been subsidized for most of the period under consideration. Second, a number of states subsidize more than one route, and the choice of routes for analysis makes a great deal of difference for the findings that result. Consequently, the analysis of routes will consider the most appropriate route (according to the transportation literature) and the least appropriate for each state that subsidizes more than one route.

In assessing the appropriateness of subsidized routes, one of the most obvious and important criteria is the population served. The larger the population served, the greater the likelihood that the route will attract significant traffic volume, other things being equal.

When the smaller of the two terminal (that is, endpoint) cities for each subsidized route is classified by the stability of state subsidy behavior, the findings are not particularly definitive. When the analysis of the stable states is confined to the routes serving the largest metropolitan areas in each state, the pattern is striking: five of the six smaller terminal cities have populations of 1.9 million or more, in contrast to only one of the routes in states that discontinued their subsidies. That pattern suggests that state terminations were guided by efficiency concerns. However, when the analysis of the stable states is confined to the subsidized routes serving smaller population centers (the least favorable comparison), the stable state routes are very similar to the routes in states that have terminated their subsidy programs.[26]

Similarly ambiguous findings result when the lengths of subsidized routes are compared. We have noted that when travel time to and from terminals is taken into account, as routes grow longer, the speed advantage of air travel grows more and more pronounced. Passenger train routes that cover short-to-intermediate distances, consequently, are more likely to be competitive in terms of travel times.[27]

Once again, comparison of stable subsidy states with states that have terminated their subsidies depends greatly on which routes from the stable states are included. If the longest route from each of the stable states is considered, the shortest of these—that is, those most time-competitive with air travel—tend to be in the states that terminated the subsidies. However, if the analysis is confined to the shortest route in each of the stable states (the most favorable comparison), route lengths in the stable states and the termination states are very similar.

A final aspect of route appropriateness is the availability of rail connections. Other things being equal, a route that has passenger rail connections at both ends is more likely to generate inbound and outbound traffic than is a route having rail connections at only one end.[28] Dead-end routes, therefore, should be more vulnerable to termination.

The comparisons between stable states and termination states are ambiguous. On one hand, five of the six stable states subsidize at least one route that has rail connections at both ends. However, half of the stable states also subsidize a dead-end route, a proportion that is identical to the proportion of dead-end routes in the termination states.

Overall, the comparisons of route characteristics in stable and termination states do not provide much support for the view that terminations resulted from particularly inappropriate choices of routes. Stable states are approximately as likely to have routes with small terminal cities and dead-end routes as are termination states. Moreover, unusually long routes, which are least likely to be time-competitive with air travel, tend to be found in the stable states.

Although route characteristics are not very useful for accounting for whether state subsidies survive, other possible avenues for inquiry are available. The social, economic, and political environments of state politics may help to account for the survival of some state subsidy programs and the elimination of others. For example, as noted earlier, metropolitanization is likely to produce a greater disposition toward governmental activism. Overall, more metropolitan states should provide a more supportive environment for continuation of subsidies. The evidence tends to support this perspective (see Table 4.3). Most of the highly metropolitan states continued subsidies once they were adopted, but almost all of the less metropolitan states that adopted Amtrak subsidies at some point between 1979 and 1986 later terminated them.

A second component of the socioeconomic environment, which also contains aspects of the task environment, is state population. As would be expected, analysis reveals that Amtrak subsidies are more likely to survive in more populous states. Of the subsidizing states that had 4.8 million or more residents in 1979, three-fourths continued their subsidies. In contrast, only one of the less populous subsidizing states continued its subsidy.

Degree of affluence is another important component of the socioeconomic setting. Officials in poorer states are likely to be under greater pressure to weed out some programs, especially new ones, to provide resources for more established commitments. In addition to affluence in general, a large tourism industry may encourage continuation of subsidies to help insure reliable tourist access. The evidence demonstrates that subsidies are indeed considerably more likely to survive in wealthier states and in states with higher levels of spending by tourists. The latter tendency is particularly strong: three-fourths of the subsidizing states with relatively large

Table 4.3   Socioeconomic Characteristics and Amtrak Subsidy Stability

	Stable Subsidy		Subsidy Discontinued	
Percentage metropolitan, 1978				
64% or less	14%	(1)	86%	(6)
80% or more	71%	(5)	29%	(2)
gamma = .88				
Population, 1979				
Less than 4.8 million	0%	(0)	100%	(6)
4.8 million or more	75%	(6)	25%	(2)
gamma = 1.0				
Per capita income, 1979				
Less than $8,550	17%	(1)	83%	(5)
More than $8,550	62%	(5)	38%	(3)
gamma = .79				
Spending by tourists, 1982				
Less than $3.9 billion	0%	(0)	100%	(6)
$3.9 billion or more	75%	(6)	25%	(2)
gamma = 1.0				

Sources: Statistical Abstract (Washington, DC: Bureau of the Census, 1980), 12, 20, 447; and *World Almanac* (New York: Newspaper Enterprise Association, 1983), 607–631.

tourist industries have continued their subsidies, but not one of the states with relatively small tourist industries has done so.

Although the stability of state Amtrak subsidies clearly is associated with the socioeconomic environment, ideological factors also warrant examination. Where a conservative electorate may at times permit adoption of a subsidy (an infrequent occurrence, as the previous analysis revealed), hostility to governmental activity in that climate eventually may produce a counterattack that leads to elimination of the subsidy. Again, the evidence clearly supports that possibility. States with relatively liberal electorates, as indicated by the McGovern vote in 1972, are more likely to continue subsidies than are more conservative states (see Table 4.4).

Similar conclusions emerge if the analysis is based on state party ideologies instead of the ideological leanings of the public. The pattern is consistent for both parties: subsidies in states with relatively conservative parties generally have been terminated, but subsidies in states with more liberal parties generally have endured. The relationships are not quite as strong as the findings based on electoral ideologies, but the tendencies are clear. Overall, subsidies are more likely to survive in more liberal states.

In addition, narrower policy predispositions may sometimes, but not always, work in tandem with ideological factors. When public officials confront a novel situation, they often look for an analogy to a previous

Table 4.4   Ideological Factors and Amtrak Subsidy Stability

	Stable Subsidy		Subsidy Discontinued	
Percentage for McGovern, 1972[a]				
38% or less	14%	(1)	86%	(6)
40% or more	71%	(5)	29%	(2)
gamma = .88				
Electoral conservatism[b]				
.10 or lower	83%	(5)	17%	(1)
.11 or higher	12%	(1)	88%	(7)
gamma = .94				
Republican Party ideology[c]				
1–2	17%	(1)	83%	(5)
3–5	62%	(5)	38%	(3)
gamma = .79				
Democratic Party ideology[d]				
1–3	62%	(5)	38%	(3)
4–5	17%	(1)	83%	(5)
gamma = –.79				

[a]*Congressional Quarterly Almanac* (Washington, DC: 1972), 1014.

[b]Gerald Wright, Robert Erikson, and John McIver, "Measuring State Partisanship," 478–480.

[c]Eugene McGregor, "Uncertainty and National Nominating Coalitions," *Journal of Politics* 40 (1978): 1020–1021. Low score denotes conservatism.

[d]McGregor, 1022–1023. Low score denotes liberalism.

decision that might provide guidance in responding to the new situation.[29] The environmental advantages of passenger rail service make an analogy with environmental policies a plausible choice. The evidence indicates that states with a history of environmental protection efforts are in fact more likely to continue Amtrak subsidies over time than are states without that history (see Table 4.5). All of the states lacking a previous record of environmental concern terminated their subsidies, but three-fourths of the states with a history of serious environmental concern have continued their subsidy programs.

Innovativeness, which, as we have seen, is related to whether subsidies are adopted initially, also may influence whether they endure. Where officials and the public are accustomed to the adoption of new initiatives, the inevitable process of working out kinks in a new program will seem routine. Where new initiatives are comparatively rare, the necessity to work through difficulties may lead to charges that the initial decision was a mistake. More innovative states should, therefore, be more likely to continue subsidy programs once they are begun. Analysis supports this expectation. Subsidy programs have a demonstrably higher mortality rate in states that are relatively slow to do new things (innovation scores of .48 or lower).

In view of the small number of cases for analysis and the large number of states' characteristics being examined, a definitive multivariate analysis of subsidy terminations and continuations is impossible. However, the same two variables—population and ideological climate—that emerged in the analysis of subsidy adoptions also can predict, with a high degree of accuracy, whether the subsidies survive (see Table 4.6).

The first step of the model indicates that states with smaller populations generally do not continue their Amtrak subsidies over time. A smaller

Table 4.5 Prior Policy Orientations and Amtrak Subsidy Stability

	Stable Subsidy		Subsidy Discontinued	
High environment concern[a]				
No	0%	(0)	100%	(6)
Yes	75%	(6)	25%	(2)
gamma = 1.0				
Policy innovativeness[b]				
.48 or lower	14%	(1)	86%	(6)
.52 or higher	71%	(5)	29%	(2)
gamma = .88				

[a]High environmental concern states (coded 1) ranked in the top 15 in air or water quality control expenditures, 1970–1971. Other states coded 0. *Source:* Charles Jones, "Regulating the Environment," in *Politics in the American States,* 3rd ed., ed. Herbert Jacob and Kenneth Vines (Boston: Little, Brown, 1976), 410–411.

[b]Jack Walker, "The Diffusion of Innovations Among the American States," *American Political Science Review* 63 (1969): 883.

Table 4.6   A Model of Amtrak Subsidy Stability

Premise		Result	Accuracy	Cumulative Percentage
Was state population 4.8 million or more in 1979?	NO ⟶	End subsidy (n = 6)	100%	43%
↓ YES				
Did McGovern receive at least 38% of the state's presidential vote, 1972?	NO ⟶	End subsidy (n = 2)	100%	57%
YES ⟶		Continue subsidy (n = 6)	100%	100%

Source: The format of this table is adapted from John Kingdon, *Congressmen's Voting Decisions,* 2nd ed. (New York: Harper and Row, 1981), 244, 330; and David Nice, "Amtrak in the States," *Policy Studies Journal* 11 (1983): 594.

state is likely to have a smaller pool of potential program beneficiaries and a smaller pool of taxpayers over whom costs can be spread. Prospects for program survival therefore increase in states with larger populations.

The second step of the model indicates that, of the more populous states, subsidy continuation is concentrated exclusively among those that are more liberal, although extraordinary liberalism evidently is not required: the critical threshold is quite close to the national average of ideological leanings, as measured by the McGovern vote. Overall, all of the states that subsidized Amtrak at some point in the period covered by this analysis behave as the model predicts. Although the number of cases is small, Fisher's exact test of the fit between predicted state action and actual state action indicates that the model's overall predictive power is significant at the .0004 level.

Conclusions

Although Amtrak is primarily a national system, with most of its policies determined nationally, several states have become involved in shaping the distribution of Amtrak service. Although the number of states subsidizing Amtrak never has been very large in any given year, those states include a substantial share of the nation's population. For example, the six states that funded Amtrak service continuously from 1979 through 1986 included nearly 35 percent of the nation's population. A substantial number of the nation's largest cities, including New York City, Chicago, Los Angeles, Philadelphia, Mobile, St. Louis, and New Orleans, have received state-subsidized service at some point in recent years. The scope of state

involvement is small when compared to state involvement in highway programs, but the record reveals that sustained state effort, especially with
local cooperation, can yield dramatic improvements in services and in public use of those services.[30]

Because of the small number of subsidizing states in most years and
changes in the ranks of subsidizing states from year to year, analysis of the
state subsidy decisions is difficult. North Carolina adopted a subsidy program, terminated it, and then later started a new one. Alabama, Louisiana,
and Mississippi ended their joint subsidy but agreed later to try a ninety-
day experiment in the summer of 1996. Any conclusions reached from
analyzing a small number of unstable cases must be treated with considerable caution.

The evidence indicates that a large population base encourages both the
adoption and survival of Amtrak subsidies. As noted previously, a large
population generally means a large pool of potential customers and a large
pool of taxpayers to sustain the subsidy. In addition, however, the states
with very large populations also tend to have large metropolitan areas, with
high levels of traffic congestion. Improved rail passenger service is one
way to get people off the freeways and to cope with traffic congestion.

The analysis also indicates that ideological factors influence subsidy
decisions, although the relationships tend to be less strong and less consistent than was found for population. The recent return of some conservative southern states to the ranks of the subsidizers suggests that ideological considerations may be weakening, but whether those subsidies will
survive remains to be seen.

Notes

1. *Book of the States* (Lexington, KY: Council of State Governments, 1984),
324–325, 376–377; Thomas Dye, *Politics in States and Communities,* 6th ed. (Englewood Cliffs, NJ: Prentice-Hall, 1988), 455–460.

2. Benjamin Allen and David Vellenga, "Public Financing of Railroads Under
the New Federalism: The Progress and Problems of Selected State Programs,"
Transportation Journal 23 (1983): 5–19; William Black and James Runke, *The
States and Rural Rail Preservation* (Lexington, KY: Council of State Governments,
1975); William Black, *Railroads for Rent* (Bloomington: Indiana University,
1986); David Nice, "State and Local Government Ownership of Freight Railroads," *Transportation Quarterly* 41 (1987): 587–600; John Stover, *American Railroads* (Chicago: University of Chicago, 1961), chapter 5.

3. Allen and Vellenga, 17.

4. Thomas Dye, *Politics, Economics, and the Public* (Chicago: Rand McNally,
1966); Thomas Dye, *American Federalism: Competition Among Governments*
(Lexington, MA: Lexington, 1990).

5. Jack Walker, "Innovation in State Politics," in *Politics in the American
States,* 2nd ed., ed. Herbert Jacob and Kenneth Vines (Boston: Little, Brown,
1971), 359.

6. David Nice, "The States and Passenger Rail Service," *Transportation Research* 21A (1987): 386–387; "New Service to Mobile," *Passenger Train Journal* 224 (1996): 12–13.

7. Charles Adrian, *State and Local Governments,* 4th ed. (New York: McGraw-Hill, 1976), 42–43; Charles Adrian and Charles Press, *Governing Urban America,* 5th ed. (New York: McGraw-Hill, 1977), 26–27.

8. Robert Friedman, "The Politics of Transportation," in *Politics in the American States,* 5th ed., ed. Virginia Gray, Herbert Jacob, and Robert Albritton (Glenview, IL: Scott, Foresman/Little, Brown, 1990), 538–541.

9. Donald Harper, *Transportation in America,* 2nd ed. (Englewood Cliffs, NJ: Prentice-Hall, 1982), 222.

10. Nice, "The States and Passenger Rail," 387.

11. As many as 20 to 25 million Americans are afraid to fly or unable to fly for health reasons. See Freeman Hubbard, *Encyclopedia of North American Railroading* (New York: McGraw-Hill, 1981), 6.

12. Nice, "The States and Passenger Rail," 387.

13. Frank Colcord, "Urban Transportation and Political Ideology: Sweden and the United States," in *Current Issues in Transportation Policy,* ed. Alan Altshuler (Lexington, MA: Lexington, 1979), 3, 14. The literature on ideology and state policymaking is considerable: see David Nice, *Policy Innovation in State Government* (Ames: Iowa State University, 1994), 27–32; Gerald Wright, Robert Erikson, and John McIver, "Public Opinion and Policy Liberalism in the American States," *American Journal of Political Science* 31 (1987): 980–1001.

14. Nice, "The States and Passenger Rail," 387.

15. Robert Savage, "Policy Innovativeness as a Trait of American States," *Journal of Politics* 40 (1978): 212–228; Walker, 354–387.

16. Nice, "The States and Passenger Rail," 387.

17. Not all observers agree on the environmental advantages of trains. See Harper, 239; George Hilton, *Amtrak* (Washington, DC: American Enterprise Institute, 1980), 52–53; *National Transportation Statistics* (Washington, DC: U.S. Department of Transportation, 1980), 106–113; Frank Wilner, *The Amtrak Story* (Omaha: Simmons-Boardman, 1994), 10, 110.

18. Nice, "The States and Passenger Rail," 387.

19. For discussion of the role of problems in shaping policy decisions, see George Edwards and Ira Sharkansky, *The Policy Predicament* (San Francisco: Freeman, 1978), 280–282; Robert Lineberry, *American Public Policy* (New York: Harper and Row, 1978), 60–62; Nice, *Policy Innovation,* 21–25.

20. Nice, "The States and Passenger Rail," 387.

21. For cautionary comments regarding the use of stepwise techniques, see Ronald Wonnacott and Thomas Wonnacott, *Econometrics,* 2nd ed. (New York: Wiley, 1979), 181–183, 407–410.

22. Nice, "The States and Passenger Rail," 389.

23. On the tendency for public programs to survive and grow, see George Break, *Financing Government in a Federal System* (Washington, DC: Brookings, 1980), 256–260; Herbert Kaufman, *Are Government Organizations Immortal?* (Washington, DC: Brookings, 1976).

24. See Charles Levine, ed., *Managing Fiscal Stress* (Chatham, NJ: Chatham House, 1980).

25. The subsidizers from 1979 through 1986 were Alabama, California, Florida, Illinois, Louisiana, Maryland, Michigan, Minnesota, Mississippi, Missouri, New York, North Carolina, Oregon, and Pennsylvania. Alabama, Florida, Louisiana, Maryland, Minnesota, Mississippi, North Carolina, and Oregon discontinued their subsidies. Source: *Amtrak National Train Timetables,* 1979–1986.

26. Derived from *Amtrak National Train Timetables,* 1979–1986 (Washington, DC: National Railroad Passenger Corporation); *Rand McNally Road Atlas* (Chicago: Rand McNally, 1987), 120–128; and *World Almanac* (New York: Newspaper Enterprise Association, 1983), 201, 207–252.

27. Hilton, 67.

28. David Nice, "The States and Amtrak," *Transportation Quarterly* 40 (1986): 569.

29. Jack Walker, "The Diffusion of Innovations Among the American States," *American Political Science Review* 63 (1969): 889; Richard Hofferbert and John Urice, "Small-Scale Policy: The Federal Stimulus Versus Competing Explanations for State Funding of the Arts," *American Journal of Political Science* 29 (1985): 308–329.

30. For example, see Carl Schiermeyer and L. Erik Lange, "The Dollars and Sense of the San Joaquins," *Passenger Train Journal* 134 (1989): 24–31.

5

International Amtrak

In an increasingly interdependent world, international transportation capabilities have grown more and more important. Companies that require raw materials from abroad or depend heavily on foreign markets cannot survive without sound international transportation services. Business managers in firms with subdivisions or subsidiaries all over the world need fast and dependable access to those operations. International transportation enables individuals to reach better jobs, visit friends and relatives, and enjoy cultural amenities offered by other countries. No longer is international travel exclusively the province of the very rich, nor is international travel simply a once-in-a-lifetime experience for many people.[1]

Although international transportation commonly evokes images of airplanes and ships, the automobile, bus, and passenger train account for many international trips each year around the world. This chapter will explore international services offered by the Amtrak system and the evolution of those services over time.

International Aspects of U.S. Passenger Rail Service

Over the years, America's private passenger railroads offered connections from the United States to Canada and Mexico. Travelers could choose from a variety of international routes, schedules, destinations, and accommodations during the period when private passenger rail service was most abundant generally. As private service declined, the international services declined as well, with only a few surviving the 1960s.[2]

Although the Amtrak system began its life as an exclusively domestic transportation system, it developed an international flavor early on through the use of imported technology. As noted earlier, because private passenger railroads in the United States largely stopped investing in passenger equipment by the late 1950s, much of the most advanced passenger train equipment by the 1970s existed outside the country. The most notable imported equipment included the turbo liners, the first of which came from France, and the AEM-7 locomotive, which is largely Swedish technology although built in the United States. The AEM-7 is the mainstay of Amtrak's Northeast Corridor and is capable of speeds well in excess of one hundred miles per hour. During the 1990s, a Swedish trainset capable of tilting to take curves at higher speeds and a German ICE trainset designed for high-speed operation were tested in actual service, and a Spanish Talgo trainset began regular service in the Pacific Northwest.[3]

In terms of routes, as constituted initially, Amtrak did not provide any international service at all. However, on June 22, 1972, Congress enacted a supplemental appropriations bill to provide the first international Amtrak service.[4] Since that time, Amtrak's management has experimented with varying international services, which have not shown equal durability. We will turn now to a discussion of those services and their differing fates.

Failed Experiments

Experimentation was a major feature of the early Amtrak system. The early development of international service reflected that experimental orientation. As with other experimental efforts, not all of the early attempts at providing international service were judged to be successful.

One of the first three international trains, the Pacific International, provided service between Seattle and Vancouver, British Columbia, beginning in 1972.[5] The Pacific International revived service that had been provided by the Burlington Northern Railroad in the pre-Amtrak era but that was terminated with Amtrak's creation.[6] The Pacific International offered coach and light food service on a schedule coordinated with other Amtrak service to and from Seattle, as well as connecting with Canadian passenger trains at Vancouver.

The Pacific International had several factors in its favor, including its relatively short route (156 miles), the substantial and growing populations of its terminal cities, the availability of rail connections at both terminals, and the fact that it was a revival of only recently discontinued service. However, throughout its history it remained a small train with relatively few passengers.[7] It finally was discontinued and replaced with bus service by 1981, although a revival occurred in 1995.

A second component of the early international experiments, the Inter-American, linked the United States and Mexico.[8] The Inter-American was a descendant of direct rail service between San Antonio and Mexico City, service that had ended prior to Amtrak's creation. From the outset, however, the Inter-American offered only quasi-international service; the southern terminal was Laredo, Texas, from which bus service transferred passengers a short distance to Nuevo Laredo, Mexico, and the National Railway of Mexico.

The Inter-American was a remarkably unstable operation over the years. It began as a triweekly service between Fort Worth and Laredo, but the following year found its northern terminal shifted to St. Louis. In 1976 the northern terminal was changed to Chicago, and the Inter-American began to offer daily service. In the following year service shifted back to triweekly.[9] The Inter-American suffered from relatively high financial losses during its lifetime[10] and finally was discontinued in 1981.

Crossing Borders:
Modest International Successes

Early in this century, a considerable number of passenger trains ran between various points in the northeastern United States and southeastern Canada. A variety of service types, from spartan to relatively luxurious, were offered on a number of different routes.[11] None of that service was included in the original Amtrak system, but the obvious value of international rail passenger service in such a densely populated area was soon recognized. The resulting developments have not always proceeded smoothly but do indicate the potential for international rail service.

One of the first additions to Amtrak's international service was the Montrealer (originally the Montrealer northbound and Washingtonian southbound), which connected Washington, DC, and Montreal via New York City, Connecticut, Massachusetts, and Vermont. The Montrealer's ancestry and name date back to 1924, but the service had been discontinued in the waning days of private passenger service.[12] Congressional action in 1972 led to its reinstatement later that year.[13]

The Montrealer's operation over a long distance on an overnight schedule made it the only full service international train, with sleeping cars and baggage checking, that survived for any length of time in the Amtrak system. That it did survive for a time was by no means a minor achievement. Deteriorating track in New England caused increasingly serious delays and, eventually, temporary termination of service in 1987.

The process leading to this decision was not simple. The national government contributed substantial funding to Guilford Industries, owners of the deteriorated track, but the company did not come through with sufficiently adequate improvements. Amtrak ultimately sought intervention by the Interstate Commerce Commission, which condemned the track in question to enable Amtrak to gain possession of it. Amtrak in turn sold the track to the Central of Vermont Railroad, which was expected to be a more cooperative owner. Service was restored following track repairs, but untangling the various legal controversies was a difficult matter, and service was again terminated later.[14] The Montrealer's experience was eloquent testimony to the complexity of an operation involving Amtrak, two national governments, a publicly owned Canadian passenger rail system, and a privately owned U.S. railroad spanning nine states and one Canadian province.

Amtrak also offers service between Montreal and the United States on the Adirondack, which links Montreal and New York City via Albany and upstate New York. Like the Montrealer, the Adirondack is a descendant of service that originated before World War II.[15] Unlike the Montrealer, however, the Adirondack was not part of the initial congressional effort to add international service to the Amtrak system. The modern Adirondack began operations in 1974, when the state of New York enacted a subsidy for the service.[16] State subsidy of an international transportation service stands in stark contrast to the inaccurate perspective that assigns all responsibility for international relations to the federal government.[17]

The Adirondack operates on a daylight schedule, and consequently does not offer some of the amenities, such as sleeping car service, that were provided by the Montrealer. However, the Adirondack does offer substantially shorter travel times between New York and Montreal than did the Montrealer, an advantage due in part to the Adirondack's more direct route.[18] When the U.S. Department of Transportation proposed drastic reductions in the Amtrak system in the late 1970s, the Adirondack was the only international service included in the reduced system, and even that inclusion was contingent on continued state funding.[19]

Additional service between the northeastern United States and Canada is provided by the Maple Leaf, linking New York City and Toronto. The Maple Leaf represents a revival of service offered by the New York Central Railroad in the pre-Amtrak era but discontinued before Amtrak's creation. The return of service evolved gradually, beginning in the 1970s with connecting service between Amtrak and the Canadian Pacific Railroad at Buffalo, New York. The trip required a change of trains at Buffalo—an experience that left something to be desired in the winters of upstate New York—and in 1981 the Maple Leaf instituted through service between New York City and Toronto. Like the Adirondack, the Maple Leaf is a day train offering coach and food service.

The last of the relatively stable international trains is the aptly named International, which connects Chicago and Toronto. Similar service was offered during the pre-Amtrak era but ended before Amtrak's formation. As with the Maple Leaf, the return of Chicago-Toronto service began gradually. In the 1970s limousine service connected Detroit, Michigan, and Windsor, Ontario; that service was replaced in the 1980s by a through train bypassing Detroit. The International, like the Adirondack and Maple Leaf, is a daylight coach train and, like the Adirondack, is state subsidized. The relative dominance of day coach service on the international routes is at least partly a reflection of the lower cost of coach service compared with sleeping car operations.[20] Ridership on the various international trains has not been particularly heavy over the years,[21] a circumstance that heightens the need for cost containment. Restricting service to day coach operations helps to achieve that goal.

Quasi-International Services

The Amtrak system has also experimented with services that do not feature trains crossing international boundaries but that do offer connecting bus service. As we have seen, past experience suggests the possibility that bus or limousine service might evolve into actual rail service at some point, although that outcome is far from certain.

Two of the experiments in quasi-international service have involved San Diego, the southern terminal of the busiest passenger rail corridor in the western United States.[22] The older and only surviving service links San Diego with Tijuana by bus and dates from the middle 1970s. A later experiment began in 1990 and connected San Diego with Calexico—a California border town—and Mexicali, Mexico, by bus. That service represented a modified revival of rail connections that had linked Calexico and Los Angeles in the pre-Amtrak era,[23] connections that were terminated prior to Amtrak's creation. The San Diego–Mexicali service lasted only a few years, however.

The other quasi-international link in the Amtrak system involved bus connections between Grand Forks, North Dakota, and Winnipeg, Manitoba. Immediately before Amtrak began operations, the Burlington Northern Railroad had offered passenger rail service between Grand Forks and Winnipeg as a branch of the Western Star, which linked St. Paul and Seattle. Neither the Western Star nor the Winnipeg branch survived into the Amtrak era, but for a time bus service between Winnipeg and Grand Forks offered a connection with Amtrak's Empire Builder, which provides service to Chicago, Minneapolis–St. Paul, Seattle, and Portland, Oregon. Access to Winnipeg also offered connections with passenger rail service in Canada, but the coordinated bus service is no longer available.

Variations in International Service

As the preceding discussion indicates, Amtrak continues to provide direct rail service on some international routes, but service on other routes is limited to bus connections or has been abandoned altogether. We now turn to the question of why some international routes have direct rail service while others do not. This question is one aspect of the broader issue of how Amtrak route services in general are distributed, an issue we examined in Chapter 3. As in domestic service, political factors and bureaucratic decision rules based on cost-effectiveness bear examination. In particular, size of population—linked to size of the potential pool of customers and size of traffic volume—and the relation of route lengths to time-competitiveness emerge again as influential.

By combining population and route length considerations, we can develop indicators of the traffic potential of the various international Amtrak routes (see Table 5.1). One indicator is the ratio of the smaller of each route's terminal (endpoint) cities to the length of the route. Routes with relatively large terminal cities and covering short distances receive higher scores on this measure, and the degree of variation is quite large, from a high of .83 for the Pacific International to a low of .06 for the Chicago-Winnipeg route. Higher scores should indicate higher traffic potential.

A second indicator of traffic potential is the ratio of the length of the route to the total population of major cities (including terminals) along the route. This indicator affords a somewhat more inclusive picture of probable traffic volume than simply considering the population of the smaller terminal city on each route. However, the more inclusive measure has a potential shortcoming: a route may have a very large population concentrated at one end and relatively few people at the other end, a situation likely to yield only modest traffic along the thinly populated portion of the route. One sign of the importance of that distinction can be seen in the relative positions of the two Los Angeles routes. When we consider the population of major cities on the routes, the Los Angeles–Tijuana and Los Angeles–Mexicali corridors emerge as the two strongest corridors. However, those high rankings are generated by the huge population in the Los Angeles–San Diego area. Beyond San Diego, the population base is

Table 5.1   Indicators of Traffic Potential on Amtrak's International Routes

Ratio of Population of Smaller Terminal Metropolitan Area to Route Length[a]		Ratio of Population of Major Metropolitan Areas on Route (Including Terminals) to Route Length[a]	
Pacific International	.83	Los Angeles–Tijuana	9.50
Adirondack	.74	Los Angeles–Mexicali	5.48
International	.61	Adirondack	5.40
Maple Leaf	.55	Montrealer	4.35
Montrealer	.41	Maple Leaf	3.97
Inter-American	.35	International	2.22
(Chicago–Mexico City)		Pacific International	2.18
Los Angeles–Tijuana	.28	Chicago-Winnipeg	1.41
Los Angeles–Mexicali	.14	Inter-American	1.31
Chicago-Winnipeg	.06		

[a]Population, 1980, in millions; length in hundreds of miles.

comparatively limited, which is why the two Los Angeles corridors rank near the bottom of the indicator based on the population of the smaller terminal city. Once again, the traffic potential of different routes appears to vary considerably; the score of the highest potential route (when the populations of all major cities along the route are considered) is more than six times as high as the score of the lowest potential route.

Given the somewhat inconsistent rankings of the two indicators of traffic potential, a cautious strategy would call for offering regular rail service under only the most promising conditions. In this case, that would mean offering service only if both indicators are relatively favorable. If we define a favorable rating as achieving one of the six highest scores on either indicator, we find that four routes appear in the top six for both indicators: the Adirondack (New York–Montreal), the International (Chicago-Toronto), the Maple Leaf (New York–Toronto), and the Montrealer (Washington, DC–Montreal). The other routes place in the top six only once or not at all.

A cross-tabulation of the indicators of traffic potential and Amtrak's international service confirms the close fit between the two. The four routes that rated highly on both indicators all had full rail service as of 1992. The five routes that achieved at most one high rating for traffic potential were all limited to bus service, which is less expensive, along at least part of the route, or they had lost service altogether. There is, then, a close relationship between indicators of traffic potential and whether full rail service is offered along a given route. The number of cases is small, but the probability that a relationship this close could emerge by chance is less than one in a hundred. The results of this analysis are consistent with the perspective that emphasizes bureaucratic decision rules in allocating governmental services.

Changes in the Mid-1990s

The experimental and somewhat unstable nature of Amtrak's international service was underscored in the mid-1990s by two important events. First, the Montrealer was discontinued, a victim of Amtrak's financial problems, continuing difficulties regarding track conditions, and, very possibly, the availability in major cities of alternative service on the Adirondack (which, unlike the Montrealer, was state subsidized). Much of the U.S. portion of the Montrealer was later revived by a new train that was subsidized by the state of Vermont. Bus connections from Vermont to Montreal preserved limited international service, but the international rail link ended.

The second major change of the mid-1990s was the revival of rail service between Seattle and Vancouver, British Columbia. The revival reflected the growing willingness of the state of Washington to assist passenger rail service and the growing population (and traffic) of the Seattle-Vancouver corridor. If we recalculate the indicators of traffic potential for the Seattle-Vancouver corridor using 1990 population figures, the ratio of the population of the smaller terminal metropolitan area to route length is 1.03, higher than any value in the first column of Table 5.1. The ratio of the population of all major metropolitan areas on the route to route length is 2.93. These two values are in the range of values of the routes where international rail service generally has survived. In other words, the indicators of traffic potential are substantially more favorable for the Seattle-Vancouver corridor than was the case earlier. The termination of service and its later return is consistent with the changing traffic potential of the corridor.

Conclusions

Criticizing the government is a perennial and venerable pastime of U.S. citizens. Although ample editorializing and political posturing on efficiency concerns is a staple of much of this criticism, systematic analysis of governmental efficiency remains comparatively scarce.[24] One reason for the paucity of systematic research is the difficulty of finding agreed upon measures of efficiency for many public programs, a difficulty that stems in part from disagreement regarding what we want government to do.

In the case of transportation policies, analysts can draw upon a number of well developed performance indicators—energy consumption per passenger mile or freight-ton mile, fatality rates, costs per passenger mile or freight-ton mile, and a host of others. While disagreements abound over the relative importance of different facets of transportation performance, analysts do have a number of performance measures that help to cast light on different policy options.

As for Amtrak's international service, when pressure to improve financial performance has been high, program administrators have looked to particular performance indicators as a guide to increasing revenues and/or reducing costs. The economics of rail service clearly make high traffic volume essential for cost-effective performance, an issue we will examine more closely in Chapter 7. As we have seen, the development of Amtrak's international service, closely linked to variance in traffic potential, bears the imprint of that dynamic.

Note, however, that efficiency and politics may be hard to untangle in cases like these. A large population base is more likely to yield cost-effective rail service but, at least in the U.S. portions of international routes, also means more votes in presidential and Senate elections and more seats in the House of Representatives. Disappointing large numbers of people is normally not a prudent strategy for political survival.

Notes

1. On the general importance of transportation, see Donald Harper, *Transportation in America*, 2nd ed. (Englewood Cliffs, NJ: Prentice-Hall, 1982), 4–10.

2. Lucius Beebe and Charles Clegg, *The Trains We Rode* (Berkeley, CA.: Howell-North, 1966), 885–897, 906–925, 936, 941; Harold Edmonson, *Journey to Amtrak* (Milwaukee: Kalmbach, 1972), 102.

3. Rodger Bradley, *Amtrak* (Poole, United Kingdom: Blandford, 1985), 80–96, 143–144; Karl Zimmerman, *Amtrak at Milepost 10* (Park Forest, IL: PTJ Publishing, 1981), 68; "On the Property," *Passenger Train Journal* 189 (September 1993): 24–29.

4. Zimmerman, 20.

5. Zimmerman, 20.

6. Edmonson, 102.

7. George Hilton, *Amtrak* (Washington, DC: AEI, 1980), 47–48; Zimmerman, 20.

8. Zimmerman, 20.

9. Zimmerman, 21.

10. Hilton, 47–48.

11. Beebe and Clegg, 885–887, 897, 906–941.

12. Charles Bohi, "Toasting the Montrealer," *Passenger Train Journal* 141 (September 1989): 8.

13. Bohi, 8, 9; Zimmerman, 20.

14. Bohi, 8–9.

15. Beebe and Clegg, 936.

16. Zimmerman, 20, 30.

17. Michael Shuman, "What the Framers Really Said About Foreign Policy Powers," *Intergovernmental Perspective* 16 (Spring 1990), 27–31.

18. David Nice, "Changing Program Performance: The Case of Amtrak," *Transportation Journal* 27 (Fall 1987): 43, 45.

19. Bradley, 135.

20. Hilton, 46.

21. For example, see "Amtrak Ridership Update," *Passenger Train Journal* 152 (August 1990), 16.

22. See Carl Schiermeyer and L. Erik Lange, "The Making of a Corridor," *Passenger Train Journal* 122 (February 1988): 16–21.

23. Beebe and Clegg, 741.

24. George Downs and Patrick Larkey, *The Search for Government Efficiency* (Philadelphia: Temple University, 1986).

6

Bringing Passengers on Board

As noted in Chapter 1, the decline of private passenger rail service in the United States has been attributed to a variety of causes, from changing technologies and public subsidies of other modes to railroad executives who tried to drive passengers away.[1] Although it is extremely difficult to assess the precise influence of each factor, one point is very clear: the public grew less and less inclined to travel by train from 1944 to 1970.[2] The Amtrak system thus constituted a type of experiment: could the public be persuaded to travel by train again?

Amtrak attacked several of the probable causes of declining ridership. New equipment, both passenger cars and locomotives, replaced the obsolete fleet inherited from the private railroads. Public subsidies helped to offset the funding given to road and air transportation systems for many years. A management team committed to passenger rail service and improved work rules offered the promise of greater concern for passenger needs and greater efficiency. Computerized ticketing and reservation systems and coordinated schedules increased passenger convenience.[3] Whether changes of this sort could attract passengers was very much a matter of uncertainty at Amtrak's creation.

A comparison of year-to-year changes in passenger train ridership, measured in passenger miles, in the closing years of private passenger train service and in the Amtrak era reveals a striking change: from 1945 through 1971, ridership fell in all but two years. In contrast, ridership in the Amtrak era has risen in three out of every four years. Moreover, ridership rose eight straight years between 1982 and 1990. The only comparable upward trend between 1920 and 1970 was in the period from 1938 to 1944, when the economic recovery from the Great Depression and mobilization for World War II combined to spur travel demand and curtail opportunities to travel by car or plane. Clearly the dynamics of passenger train ridership have changed in the Amtrak era.[4]

All organizations, whether public or private, need to prepare for future conditions. A transportation service that fails to anticipate rising demand will be unable to meet customer needs, particularly if added volume requires additional equipment that takes months to obtain. Overutilization of facilities to meet excess demand can produce crowding and equipment failures, neither of which is likely to please customers. Conversely, a system that fails to anticipate declining demand will have idle capacity and, in the case of a public agency, may face criticism for wasting public funds on unnecessary equipment and underutilized personnel. Organizations therefore need to be able to forecast demand levels.

From a management standpoint, a forecasting model will be more useful if it is based on predictors that the organization can control and/or predictors for which forecasted values are readily available. For example, the federal government and a number of other organizations regularly produce forecasts of future economic activity; those forecasts generally are quite accurate, although exceptions do occur.[5]

The following analysis will seek to develop a model to explain Amtrak ridership nationwide. Although a nationwide model obviously will be of scant value for making route-specific decisions, the increasing emphasis on overall totals in the federal budget process[6] makes a national model potentially valuable. In the context of persisting concern about federal budget deficits, improved ability to forecast overall traffic volume will be useful for predicting total program costs. In addition, a national model may be useful in making decisions regarding overall system capacity and as a supplement to existing models for assessing demand on individual routes.[7]

Influences on Ridership

Research on transportation generally, and Amtrak specifically, identifies a number of possible influences on ridership. Not all of the studies are consistent, but taken together they suggest useful avenues of inquiry.

One of the most obviously determining factors governing ridership is the system's ability to keep reasonably on schedule. Amtrak's on-time performance has been a point of significant concern over the years. In fiscal year 1978, failure to meet schedules was the single most frequent complaint on passenger response forms.[8] On-time performance is affected by many factors, from weather and mechanical problems to the cooperativeness of the railroad owning the track,[9] but whatever the cause of the delay, late trains are likely to produce unhappy customers. A note of caution may be in order, however: time concerns may differ according to the purpose of travel.[10] Business passengers are likely to regard delays in terms of missed appointments, irritated customers, and angry employers. However, to the degree that many Amtrak passengers are traveling for relatively leisure-oriented purposes,[11] on-time performance may be a less determining influence on ridership.

A second possible influence on ridership is the reach of the Amtrak system, as indicated by the number of train miles per year. Train miles are increased by providing service on more routes or by providing more frequent service on an existing route. On balance, increasing train miles should help to increase ridership. Available evidence clearly indicates that more frequent service achieves this.[12]

A third potential influence on travel generally and Amtrak ridership specifically is the economic climate. When the economy is performing poorly, recreational travel is a luxury that many people cannot afford. A faltering economy also may cause companies to curtail business travel, both to conserve scarce funds and because there may be fewer reasons to travel (for example, if customers place orders less often).[13] The economy may be particularly important for Amtrak because much of its traffic involves relatively discretionary travel, which can be postponed or cancelled if people feel uncertain about their financial situations.[14]

Two aspects of the economy merit examination. First, the gross national product, adjusted for inflation, is probably the broadest available measure of overall economic activity. A larger gross national product brings more business activity and more people with the ability to afford leisure travel. Second, the unemployment rate provides a relatively visible indicator of economic performance, although the unemployment of some people may not necessarily influence the travel decisions of other people.

A fourth possible influence on Amtrak ridership is the cost of Amtrak travel borne by the customers. Other things being equal, when travelers have numerous options, the cost of traveling by any single mode or carrier is likely to be a powerful influence on their choices. That may be particularly true for Amtrak, many of whose passengers are traveling for recreational purposes. Discretionary travel of this type can be shifted to other modes but also may be postponed or cancelled entirely if costs are too high.[15]

Assessing the costs borne by Amtrak's customers presents a number of complications. Assessment must take into account varying accommodations (coach or sleeping car), discount versus full-price fares, and varying customer expenditures on meals and snacks. A useful general indicator of customer cost is Amtrak's operating revenue per passenger mile (adjusted for inflation). Although some of Amtrak's operating revenues are not transportation related but derived from real estate operations and other activities, these revenues are a comparatively small share of the total (less than 15 percent in 1988).[16] They may weaken slightly the apparent relationship between revenues and passenger volume but otherwise should present few problems for the analysis.

A final potential influence on Amtrak ridership is its rolling stock. Most travelers are concerned with the quality of transportation services to one degree or another. Equipment that is obviously worn and in shabby condition is unattractive in an aesthetic sense and may raise concerns about its mechanical reliability. Moreover, mechanical problems in aging equipment may produce failures in climate control systems or lighting or may cause an uncomfortable ride. None of those results is likely to please travelers.[17]

Concern for the passenger car fleet has been a major focus of the Amtrak system throughout its history. When it began operations with its fleet of inherited old cars,[18] failures of climate control systems generated many passenger complaints,[19] and the appearance of the equipment on some routes suggested an enterprise on the verge of collapse. As we saw in Chapter 2, by purchasing new equipment and by extensively rebuilding older cars, Amtrak has improved its fleet's appearance, mechanical reliability, and ride quality; but because of capital budget fluctuations, improvements have been difficult to sustain over the years.

Analysis of ridership on some routes indicates that new equipment may be helpful in attracting and retaining customers, other things being equal.[20] A historical perspective may be cautionary, however. In the period after World War II, U.S. railroads invested in a wide variety of new passenger equipment, from dome cars and observation cars to sleeping accommodations with greater comfort and privacy. Climate control systems, suspension systems, and even seats were modernized to improve reliability and passenger comfort. In spite of that investment, ridership continued to decline.[21] In the broad scheme of things, then, new equipment may be at best a modest influence on ridership.

Analysis

The zero-order relationships between Amtrak passenger volume and various possible influences on it are consistent with some of the preceding hypotheses, but others receive little or no support (see Table 6.1). On-time performance systemwide is essentially unrelated to passenger volume. This finding may reflect variations in on-time performance from one route to another but may also reflect the possibility that train passengers are somewhat less concerned about travel time than are auto or particularly airplane travelers. At any rate, fluctuations in on-time performance are of no value in accounting for variations in ridership.

The number of train miles generated annually by the Amtrak system is, in contrast, associated modestly with passenger volume and in the expected direction. Whether train miles are increased by instituting more routes or by offering more frequent service on existing routes, the result is greater availability of service and somewhat higher traffic volume.

Table 6.1 Amtrak Passenger Volume, 1972–1988: Zero-Order Relationships

	Amtrak Passenger Miles[a]
Percent of trains on time	.02
Train miles	.42*
Real gross national product[b]	.88**
Unemployment rate	−.07
Real operating revenue per passenger mile[b]	.55*
Average age of passenger cars	−.55*

[a]Intercity traffic only.
[b]In 1982 dollars; the GNP deflator is used to correct for inflation.
*Significant at the .05 level. N = 17.
**Significant at the .01 level.

Economic factors produce mixed results in accounting for Amtrak ridership. Real gross national product is related quite strongly to passenger volume (r = .88), a finding consistent with the contention that higher levels of economic activity generally produce greater traffic volume. In contrast, the unemployment rate is essentially unrelated to passenger volume. As noted earlier, the unemployment of some people (a proportionally small number for the years examined here) may have little or no impact on the travel decisions of others, whether these decisions involve either business or pleasure.

Contrary to expectations, operating revenues per passenger mile are associated positively with Amtrak ridership. There is little doubt that certain highly priced commodities—luxury automobiles for example—are purchased in part to display the consumer's affluence or social status. However, train travel in the United States does not appear to fit in the same category as fur coats, fine jewelry, or Rolls Royces. Subsequent analysis will reveal that this finding is due to the influence of another variable.

Finally, the average age of the passenger car fleet is related negatively to ridership, as expected. Obsolete equipment with unreliable climate control systems and a generally decrepit appearance is hardly inviting to the traveling public and appears not to generate much repeat business.

Because of the large number of predictors relative to the number of cases, stepwise multiple regression analysis was used to develop a parsimonious model to predict Amtrak ridership (see Table 6.2). All of the predictors in Table 6.1 were eligible for inclusion in the model. In addition, re-estimation using backward elimination produced identical results. Finally, when all variables were transformed by taking the common logarithm of each value, the results were virtually identical to the findings in Table 6.2.

The multivariate findings confirm the single strongest zero-order finding: a higher level of gross national product is associated with higher

Table 6.2   Regression Analysis of Amtrak Passenger Volume[a]

	b	beta	t	Significance
Real gross national product[b]	1.68	1.22	6.98	.000
Real operating revenue per passenger mile[c]	−1.10	−.42	−2.41	.031
Intercept	50.28	—	1.08	.301
R^2 = .84				
Durbin and Watson's d = 1.81				

[a]Passenger miles in tens of millions (intercity traffic only).
[b]In tens of billions of 1982 dollars.
[c]In tenths of a cent, in 1982 cents.

levels of ridership. Specifically, a $10 billion dollar real increase in the gross national product is associated with a ridership increase of nearly 17 million passenger miles. In addition, real operating revenues per passenger mile are related negatively to ridership once the gross national product is taken into account. For each tenth of a cent increase in revenues per passenger mile, ridership falls by approximately 11 million passenger miles. The model is able to account for nearly 85 percent of the variance in Amtrak ridership and is free of significant autocorrelated error problems.

A comparison of the actual levels of Amtrak ridership and the levels predicted by the model in Table 6.2 confirms the close correspondence between the two (see Table 6.3). The fit between the actual and predicted values is quite close for the period from 1979 through 1988; none of the prediction errors exceeds 4 percent of the actual value for that year. The model's performance is somewhat less impressive in the earlier years, in part because of the 1974 oil embargo and in part because of Amtrak's general instability in its early years,[22] a fairly common phenomenon in new organizations.

The model correctly predicts the decline in ridership from 1981 to 1982 and the sustained increase in ridership from 1982 through 1988. In addition, the model correctly identifies 1976 as the year that ridership would exceed four billion passenger miles and 1986 as the year that passenger volume would exceed five billion passenger miles. As a final check, the coefficients from Table 6.2 were used to predict 1989 ridership, based on the real gross national product and real operating revenue per passenger mile in 1989. The resulting prediction of 5,572 million passenger miles is within 5 percent of actual ridership (5,859 million passenger miles) for that year.

The results of the statistical analysis are consistent with the view that transportation demand is influenced heavily by broader economic forces. When the economy booms, business travel expands and people can afford recreational travel. When the economy falters, travel plans are likely to be

Table 6.3   Predicted and Actual Amtrak Ridership

	Actual Value[a]	Predicted Value[b]
1972	304	348
1973	381	376
1974	426	368
1975	394	385
1976	422	410
1977	433	430
1978	403	456
1979	492	477
1980	458	468
1981	476	474
1982	417	419
1983	425	436
1984	455	451
1985	482	486
1986	501	509
1987	522	522
1988	568	546

[a]Passenger miles in tens of millions (intercity only).
[b]Based on equation in Table 6.2.

curtailed or postponed. The sluggish economy in the early 1990s helps explain the leveling off of Amtrak passenger volume during that period. The Amtrak system has been successful in capturing a share of the travel activity generated by prosperity. In contrast, private passenger trains after World War II experienced declining ridership even in years when the economy was expanding.

In addition, however, the findings confirm earlier evidence that Amtrak travelers are sensitive to price concerns. When much of the traffic is discretionary travel, higher prices may cause a shift to other modes or a cutback in travel plans.[23] On all major corridors, Amtrak faces stiff competition from both air- and highway-based transportation modes. In that context, unattractive Amtrak fares will yield a loss of customers to that competition.

Conclusions

In the period following World War II, the U.S. economy expanded considerably, although occasional recessions occurred. U.S. railroads invested enormous sums in new passenger equipment, primarily in the late 1940s and 1950s. The railroads experimented with a variety of techniques to attract passengers: discount fares, low-priced meals, and even fashion shows on some trains from New York to Florida. In spite of those developments, passenger train ridership declined steadily from 1945 through 1971.

The Amtrak system has succeeded in stopping the decline in passenger train ridership and has generated modest but relatively steady increases in ridership since 1972. Between 1972 and 1991, passenger miles increased by 106 percent. Nothing remotely comparable occurred during private operation of passenger trains in the postwar era.

In the broadest sense the results of this analysis confirm the view that passengers can be attracted to passenger trains. Amtrak's management has pursued a variety of strategies to enhance the appeal and convenience of train travel; modernization of equipment, improved ticketing and reservation systems, and nationwide and regional advertising campaigns are among the tactics that have been employed to boost ridership.[24] The combined effect of these efforts is clear. The Amtrak system has been able to tap some of the growing travel demand generated by an expanding economy and competitive prices, an achievement unmatched by private U.S. passenger trains since World War II.

Notes

1. For discussions of the decline, see Hilton, *Amtrak* (Washington, DC: American Enterprise Institute, 1980), 3–11; Peter Lyon, *To Hell in a Day Coach* (Philadelphia: Lippincott, 1968); David Morgan, "Who Shot the Passenger Train?" *Trains* 19 (1959): 14–51.

2. Hilton, 2–5.

3. David Nice, "Stability of the Amtrak System," *Transportation Quarterly* 43 (1989): 557–570.

4. Ridership figures are from George Hilton, *Amtrak* (Washington, DC: American Enterprise Institute, 1980), 3–4; Roger Bradley, *Amtrak* (Poole, United Kingdom: Blandford Press, 1985), 123; *Annual Report* (Washington, DC: National Railroad Passenger Corporation, 1986 and 1990).

5. Edwin Mansfield, *Statistics for Business and Economics*, 2nd ed. (New York: Norton, 1983), 548–549.

6. Aaron Wildavsky, *The New Politics of the Budgetary Process* (Glenview, IL: Scott, Foresman, 1988), 93, 425–426.

7. See Hilton, 41–42; James Sloss and James Kneafsey, "The Demand for Intercity Rail Travel: A Comparison of the British and American Experiences," *Transportation Journal* 16 (1977): 71–80.

8. *Report to the President and the Congress: Effectiveness of the Act: Amtrak* (Washington, DC: Interstate Commerce Commission, 1979), 7.

9. *Report to the President*, 12–13.

10. M. E. Beesley, "The Value of Time Spent in Travelling: Some New Evidence," in *The Demand for Travel: Theory and Measurement*, ed. Richard Quandt (Lexington, MA: Heath Lexington Books, 1970), 221–234.

11. The purposes for which people travel by train vary by route. See Hilton, 38–39.

12. See Hilton, 39–42; Richard Quandt and William Baumol, "The Demand for Abstract Transport Modes: Theory and Measurement," in *The Demand for Travel: Theory and Measurement*, ed. Richard Quandt (Lexington, MA: Heath Lexington Books, 1970), 86–90.

13. Martin Farris and Forrest Harding, *Passenger Transportation* (Englewood Cliffs, NJ: Prentice-Hall, 1976), 70, 77; *Report to the President*, 36.

14. Hilton, 38–39; Farris and Harding, 77.

15. Farris and Harding, 71–72, 77; Sloss and Kneafsey, 74–75.

16. See *Annual Report* (Washington, DC: National Railroad Passenger Corporation, 1988), 8, 24.

17. See Farris and Harding, 73–78, for a discussion of quality concerns.

18. Rodger Bradley, *Amtrak* (Poole, United Kingdom: Blandford, 1985), 41, 64; Inez Morris and David Morris, *North America by Rail* (Indianapolis: Bobbs-Merrill, 1977), 206–212.

19. *Report to the President*, 7.

20. Hilton, 39–42.

21. John Stover, *The Life and Decline of the American Railroad* (New York: Oxford University, 1970), 214–218.

22. Karl Zimmerman, *Amtrak at Milepost 10* (Park Forest, IL: PTJ Publishing, 1981), 3.

23. Hilton, 36–37.

24. Nice, "Stability," 557–570.

7

<hr>

The Balance Sheet

In recent years scholars and practitioners have produced a virtual torrent of literature on the intermingled issues of governmental efficiency, effectiveness, and productivity. Interest in these issues has been generated by rising government costs, inflation and other economic problems, revenue scarcity, and public cynicism regarding governmental performance. Studies have emerged that offer recommendations for improving efficiency, effectiveness, and productivity,[1] although some observers are skeptical of many diagnoses of public sector operations and proposals for change.[2]

Productivity is critical to a nation's standard of living and is one of the most central of all management tasks.[3] It typically includes both efficiency and effectiveness. Most observers regard efficiency as the ratio of benefits to costs; effectiveness represents output or achievement relative to some goal or performance standard.[4] Improving performance, therefore, requires increasing the ratio of benefits to costs and/or increasing progress toward some goal. Benefits, costs, and performance standards are not always easily measured and are sometimes controversial,[5] but those difficulties are not universal. This chapter will analyze the financial performance of the Amtrak system over the years.

Certain approaches to industrial productivity have generally emphasized the amount or value of production relative to the amount of labor input. Analyses of agriculture, on the other hand, might focus on production relative to the amount of land under cultivation. Still other studies examine the relationship between production and capital equipment. Because a variety of factors may influence productivity, no single indicator of it is likely to be ideal. However, analyzing the total costs of producing a good or service provides an overall indication of productivity when compared to the amount or value of the good or service produced.[6]

Amtrak provides a valuable test case for assessing productivity in several respects. First, a number of observers have charged that Amtrak does not provide benefits sufficient to justify its costs and that it is subsidized disproportionately,[7] an issue we will explore in Chapter 8. The system's financial performance has been a point of controversy throughout its existence, and Amtrak's management has established goals of increasing revenues, containing costs, and ultimately achieving financial self-sufficiency,[8] with the exception of capital equipment costs.

In addition, Amtrak is a useful test case because it operates in a competitive environment. Critics often contend that public agencies have little incentive to improve their financial performance because they are monopolies.[9] The competitive environment of passenger transportation may give the Amtrak system a greater incentive to improve its performance than is the case for many agencies.[10]

Finally, the Amtrak system has a number of performance indicators that can be measured readily, unlike some other programs. It participates in market activities that help to generate information on the relative benefits and costs of its services,[11] although not all consequences of transportation decisions are reflected in market transactions. Evidence of Amtrak's financial performance is easily available; clearly that performance has varied considerably over the years.[12] We now turn to a discussion of what might cause that variation.

Influences on Financial Performance

A great many factors can affect an organization's financial performance, from the motivation of the organization's personnel and the skill of its managers to technology, client reactions, and even luck.[13] The task of selecting a manageable number of possible factors for analysis is a difficult but vital task. The following hypotheses are not exhaustive but do cover a substantial range of possible influences.

One of the most obvious possibilities is that Amtrak's equipment affects its financial performance, although the nature of the relationship is difficult to predict. As we have seen, heavy investment by U.S. railroads in new passenger equipment after World War II failed to stem financial losses for passenger rail service,[14] but, more recently, evidence indicates that new equipment has generated increased Amtrak ridership on individual routes.[15] Whether financial performance also improves remains to be seen.

A very different perspective on equipment investment indicates that it is likely to have an adverse effect on financial performance. According to this perspective, public officials (and private managers as well) often emphasize short-run considerations at the expense of longer-term concerns. When revenues are scarce, postponing new investment can produce large short-term savings and improve short-term performance (depending on how the investment is financed), but the short-term advantages of postponing modernization are likely to be modest. The long-term problems that result from failing to modernize are borne by a later group of officials, in all likelihood.[16]

A second major influence on performance is the life cycle of an organization. A newly created organization is likely to include a substantial number of people who are not entirely familiar with their responsibilities. People who do not know one another have not had the opportunity to develop smooth working relationships or confidence in one another. Some policies and procedures may be inappropriate at first; inexperience is likely to yield strategic and tactical errors. With time and experience, people gain skills. Policies and procedures are refined and improved as experience accumulates, and working relationships develop gradually. The life cycle perspective, then, predicts that a new organization is likely to perform poorly at first but gradually will improve as experience and skills develop and unanticipated problems are resolved.[17]

The life cycle perspective appears to be consistent with some descriptions of Amtrak's history. Amtrak was created with considerable haste and amid considerable uncertainty regarding its form. Much of the equipment was in worse condition than anticipated, and incompatibility of equipment from different railroads created operational and maintenance problems. Early efforts to develop state-of-the-art passenger locomotives were only partially successful. The Amtrak system was embroiled in controversies regarding its mission, route structure, and very existence. With time and considerable effort, however, Amtrak developed a stable route structure, greater managerial control over operations, and a more modern and interchangeable equipment fleet.[18] Coming into maturity as an organization might well be related, in these respects, to better financial performance.

A third possible influence on Amtrak's financial performance is the price of the service. The nature of the relationship is difficult to predict, however. At first glance we might expect that a service operating at a loss would reduce those losses by raising prices, both to increase revenues for services provided and to minimize money-losing services (for example, if sleeping car service loses money, raising prices might reduce consumption to the point that a heavily used train could get by with just one sleeping car instead of two). However, the overall effect of price changes may depend on customer response. In a competitive passenger transportation market, an increase in prices may lead to great loss of business, resulting in poorer financial performance.[19] Available evidence indicates that Amtrak passengers are fairly sensitive to price increases and will travel less by train as prices rise.[20]

A final possible influence on Amtrak's financial performance is traffic volume. The principle of economies of scale holds that greater production or volume of activity will lead to lower average costs as fixed costs are distributed more broadly, facilities are utilized more fully, and specific

tasks (such as heavy overhaul work on locomotives or getting baggage off
a train rapidly at a particular station stop) are performed frequently enough
to become familiar to service providers and permit specialization. Beyond
a certain point, however, increasing the scale of operations can lead to bot-
tlenecks, resource shortages, and problems of organizational communica-
tion and control, with the result that average costs begin to rise.[21]

In the case of Amtrak, the literature offers fairly clear guidance on the
expected relationship between financial performance and traffic volume.
Rail transportation has relatively high fixed costs, because of required investments in right of way, rolling stock, and other facilities.[22] To the degree that sharing large fixed costs more broadly yields declining average
costs,[23] the Amtrak system should display economies of scale and therefore have better financial performance with greater traffic volume. Research on local transportation programs points to the same conclusion.[24]

Data and Methods

Financial performance can be measured in countless ways, but two fundamental indicators have figured prominently in Amtrak's history. The first
is the proportion of Amtrak's expenses that are covered by its own revenues (that is, excluding subsidies). Amtrak's management has established
the goal of making the system financially self-sufficient by the year
2000.[25] Analyzing variation in the proportion of expenses covered by system revenues may cast light on factors influencing progress toward that
goal. Clearly the revenue/expense ratio has fluctuated considerably over
the years. The ratio exceeded .50 during Amtrak's first three years of operation but then declined to a low point of .37 in 1978. Steady improvement in the revenue/cost ratio began in 1980, with the ratio rising from .39
in that year to .80 in 1993, followed by a slight decline to .77 in 1994.

A second indicator of financial performance is the net loss (the difference between revenues and expenses) per passenger mile. This measure
must be adjusted for inflation; the GNP deflator was used for that purpose.
Here, too, performance has varied substantially over the years. Amtrak's
net loss per passenger mile (in 1982 dollars) was 8.8¢ in its first year but
gradually rose to just over 18¢ in 1978. A steady decline began in 1983,
with the net loss per passenger mile falling from 18.3¢ to 9.0¢ in 1989, rising slightly to 10.2¢ in 1990, then slowly declining to 9.5¢ in 1993. Not
surprisingly, the two measures of financial performance are strongly cor-
related but not identical ($r = -.76$ for the period from 1972 through 1989).

The state of Amtrak's equipment will be measured by the average age
of Amtrak's cars and locomotives. Age obviously is only an approximate
indicator of the condition of equipment; maintenance plays a major role
in equipment performance.[26] Nevertheless, older equipment is likely to

generate higher maintenance costs and greater risk of equipment problems. On the other hand, a relatively new equipment fleet will entail substantial purchase costs initially.

The life cycle hypothesis will be assessed by the number of years that the Amtrak system has existed. The literature is not clear on the precise configuration of the relationship between time and system development. Consequently, scatterplots were examined in addition to the analysis reported subsequently. A dummy variable for changes in Amtrak's accounting methods in 1978 also was explored but proved to have no independent influence on Amtrak's financial performance or on any of the findings in this analysis.

Amtrak's prices present a significant measurement problem in light of the variety of fares and accommodations from which travelers may choose. A relatively broad measure is the system's operating revenue per passenger mile (adjusted for inflation using the GNP deflator). As has been noted, this measure includes a modest amount of revenue generated by nonpassenger operations, but that revenue never has comprised more than a small fraction of Amtrak's total operating revenue.

Two measures of Amtrak's traffic volume will be used to test the economies/diseconomies of scale hypotheses. First, the number of passenger miles generated by the Amtrak system provides a relatively broad measure of total volume. A problem with this measure, however, is that a system running a large number of lightly used trains could generate many passenger miles but in a very inefficient manner. A somewhat more useful indicator of volume, therefore, may be passenger miles per train mile. This approach affords more precise information on how broadly the fixed costs of running a typical train can be distributed.

Analysis

The zero-order relationships between the independent variables and Amtrak's financial performance are consistent with most of the hypotheses, although some of the relationships are rather weak (see Table 7.1). Moreover, a number of the relationships are quite different when financial performance is measured by revenues as a percentage of expenses rather than by net loss per passenger mile.

One version of the capital investment hypotheses is substantially supported in two cases and modestly supported in a third. Net losses per passenger mile tend to be lower when the average ages of the car fleet and locomotive fleet are higher. In addition, revenues as a percentage of costs tend to be higher when the average locomotive is older. However, the average age of the car fleet is essentially unrelated to the revenue/expense ratio. Overall, the findings are broadly consistent with the perspective that

Table 7.1　Financial Performance of Amtrak: Zero-Order Relationships

	Revenues as a Percentage of Expenses	Net Losses per Passenger Mile
Average age of cars	−.11	−.42*
Average age of locomotives	.27	−.72**
Age of organization	.56**	.00
Operating revenue per passenger mile	.80**	−.24
Passenger miles	.47*	−.14
Passenger miles per train mile	.66*	−.32

*Significant at the .05 level, one-tailed test. N = 18; data cover from 1972 through 1989.
**Significant at the .01 level.

investment in new equipment yields poor financial performance in the short run.

The life cycle hypothesis is supported in one instance but not the other. Revenues as a percentage of expenses have tended to rise over time, but net losses per passenger mile show no clear secular trend. The price hypothesis fares somewhat better: higher operating revenues per passenger mile are associated strongly with a higher revenue/expense ratio (r = .80) and are associated modestly with lower net losses per passenger mile. Higher service prices, in this case, lead to improved economic performance.

Finally, the evidence supports the economies of scale hypothesis. Higher passenger miles, particularly relative to train miles, are associated with higher revenues relative to costs and lower net losses per passenger mile, although the relationships with net losses are comparatively modest in strength. In an activity with substantial capital investment requirements, greater volume yields improved financial performance.

Multivariate analysis with only eighteen cases (the eighteen years covered by the analysis) is a somewhat perilous enterprise, but multiple regression of Amtrak's financial performance yields relatively clear results. Analysis of the ratio of Amtrak's revenues to expenses indicates that three factors are related substantially to the revenue/expense ratio (see Table 7.2). The ratio tends to be higher when revenues per passenger mile are higher, when the locomotive fleet is older, and when passenger miles per train mile are greater. Passenger miles per train mile tells us, roughly, how many passengers a typical train is carrying while covering an average mile. Given substantial fixed costs (crew, locomotive, cars, fuel, etc.) for running a train, if the average train typically carries few passengers, it will lose a lot of money. Higher prices and higher volume, then, yield an improved revenue/cost ratio, as does aging equipment. None of the other predictors has any noticeable degree of predictive power.

Overall, the regression analysis is able to explain over 95 percent of the variance in the revenue/cost ratio. When backward elimination is used to remove independent variables that have virtually no predictive power, the three-variable model that results has predictive power virtually identical to that of the full model, and the three coefficients for the predictors in the restricted model are broadly similar to their counterparts in the full model, with the partial exception of passenger miles per train mile. Moreover, the three-variable model is quite free of autocorrelation problems, as indicated by the Durbin-Watson test.

When analysis shifts to net losses per passenger mile, the age of the locomotive fleet again emerges as a significant predictor, with an older fleet associated with lower losses (see Table 7.3). In addition, more passenger miles per train mile are associated with lower losses, as predicted by the economies of scale perspective. Once again the predictive power is quite high, and the analysis is free of autocorrelation problems.

When backward elimination is used to remove independent variables that have virtually no predictive power, the explanatory power of the resulting model is virtually identical to the full model. The coefficients for

Table 7.2 Regression Analysis of Amtrak Revenues as a Percentage of Expenses

	Full Model	Restricted Model
Average age of cars	.36	—
Average age of locomotives	1.10*	1.34**
Time	57	—
Operating revenue per passenger mile	2.62*	3.26**
Passenger miles	−.08	—
Passenger miles per train mile	.38*	.17**
Accounting dummy	−.86	
Intercept	−24.8	−28.7**
R^2	.97	.96
Durbin-Watson test	2.58	2.01

Note: Coefficients are unstandardized regression coefficients.
*Significant at the .05 level.
**Significant at the .01 level.

Table 7.3 Regression Analysis of Net Losses per Passenger Mile (net of inflation)

	Full Model	Restricted Model
Average age of cars	−.18	—
Average age of locomotives	−.55*	−.66**
Time	−.18	
Operating revenue per passenger mile	.07	
Passenger miles	.02	
Passenger miles per train mile	−.16	−.11**
Accounting dummy	.34	
Intercept	36.31**	36.40**
R^2	.91	.90
Durbin-Watson test	2.42	2.15

*Significant at the .05 level.
**Significant at the .005 level.

the two predictors that emerge are quite similar to their counterparts in the full model as well.

The multivariate findings in both cases support the view that passenger rail service, with its high fixed costs, is most cost effective with high traffic volume. As passenger miles per train mile rise, the revenue-to-expense ratio rises and losses per passenger mile decline. Both multivariate analyses indicate that older equipment, as indicated by the age of the locomotive fleet, is associated with better financial performance. That is scarcely a viable strategy over the long run, for older equipment eventually brings greater maintenance costs and greater risk of breakdowns, but the findings do indicate a conflict between equipment modernization and financial performance, as indicated by published statistics. Finally, higher revenues per passenger mile are associated with a higher revenue/expense ratio but are essentially unrelated to losses per passenger mile.

Improved Financial Performance
and a Perspective on Self-Sufficiency

The results of the regression analysis can be used to assess the relative contributions of different factors to the recent improvements in Amtrak's financial performance. From 1982 to 1989, Amtrak's revenue/expense ratio rose from 47 percent to 72 percent, and its net loss per passenger mile (adjusted for inflation with the GNP deflator and with 1982 dollars as the base) fell from 18.3¢ in 1983 to 9.0¢ in 1989. The preceding analysis can help to cast light, at least in a tentative fashion, on the roots of those changes. The results of this exercise depend somewhat on whether coefficients from the full models or restricted models are used.

For example, all of the regression findings indicate that an older locomotive fleet is associated with better financial performance. From 1982 to 1989, the average age of Amtrak's locomotives rose from four years to eleven years. By multiplying the seven year age increase by the regression coefficients from Table 7.2 and Table 7.3, we can make a statistical estimate of the financial improvement that resulted. The full model coefficient from Table 7.2 indicates that a seven-year increase in the fleet's age would yield a predicted improvement in the revenue/cost ratio of 7.7 percentage points (7×1.1). That constitutes approximately 31 percent of the observed improvement of 25 percentage points. The full model coefficient from Table 7.3 indicates that the six year increase in the locomotive fleet's age from 1983 through 1989 yields an expected 3.3¢ decrease in Amtrak's net loss per passenger mile ($6 \times -.55$). That is approximately 35 percent of the observed 9.3¢ decrease in the net loss per passenger mile. These findings indicate that roughly one-third of the improvement in Amtrak's financial performance during the 1980s was due to equipment aging (using the coefficients from the restricted models would assign a somewhat larger share of the improvement to equipment aging).

A parallel analysis of the role of traffic volume (passenger miles per train mile, which rose from 144 in 1982 and 146 in 1983 to 188 in 1989) indicates that, using the full model coefficients, the 44 passenger miles per train mile increase from 1982 to 1989 yields a predicted increase in the revenue/cost ratio of 16.7 percentage points (44 × .38). That increase is fully 67 percent of the observed increase of 25 percentage points. In a similar fashion, the 42 passenger miles per train mile increase from 1983 to 1989 yields a predicted 6.7¢ decrease in net losses per passenger mile (42 × −.16). That is 72 percent of the observed decrease of 9.3¢ for that period. Overall the findings indicate that increased passenger volume has been a powerful contributer to Amtrak's improved financial performance (using coefficients from the restricted models would assign a smaller share of the improvement to traffic volume).

This type of analysis also can be used to estimate what would be needed to make Amtrak financially self-sufficient. In 1989, Amtrak's revenues covered 72 percent of its costs. The full regression results indicate that an increase of one passenger mile per train mile is associated with a .38 percentage point increase in the percentage of costs covered by Amtrak's revenues. Covering all of Amtrak's costs in 1989 would have required increasing the ratio by 28 percentage points. Solving the equation .38 × X = 28 yields a solution of 74 passenger miles per train mile. Adding that figure to the actual 1989 ridership figure of 188 passenger miles per train mile yields a total of 262 passenger miles per train mile, the load that, based on the analysis, would bring the system to financial self sufficiency.

A parallel analysis using net loss per passenger mile for 1989 yields similar findings. Amtrak's net loss per passenger mile in 1989 was 9.0¢. The full model results indicated that an increase of one passenger mile per train mile would yield an expected reduction of 0.16¢ in the net loss per passenger mile. Solving the equation −.16 × X = 9.0 yields a solution of 56.25 passenger miles per train mile. Adding that to the actual 1989 ridership produces a total of 244.25 passenger miles per train mile, the load needed to reduce expected losses to zero.

Extrapolation well beyond observed values involves a great deal of risk, for relationships may change shape in unknown ways beyond observed values. Moreover, such an exercise assumes that all else remains constant. Nevertheless, both of the above extrapolations yield fairly similar results: passenger loadings of 244 to 262 passenger miles per train mile systemwide are associated with predictions of financial self-sufficiency. That would be the equivalent of six or seven fully occupied Heritage Fleet coaches or as few as four fully occupied Superliner coaches.

Conclusions

Increasing the efficiency, effectiveness, and productivity of government has been a major concern in recent years, but overly simplistic comments and glib generalizations have greatly outnumbered systematic analyses in much of the public discussion.[27] Reasonably dependable research findings on factors that affect program performance remain scarce, although not as scarce as was the case in the early 1960s.

The financial performance of the Amtrak system has been a point of substantial controversy over the years. That performance has varied considerably, however; the percentage of Amtrak's costs covered by its revenues has ranged from as little as 37 percent to as high as 80 percent. Amtrak's loss per passenger mile, net of inflation, has ranged from 7.6¢ to 18.3¢. The preceding analysis has tried to explain those variations.

The findings strongly confirm the belief that rail service has economies of scale: higher levels of ridership are associated with stronger financial performance. Higher operating revenues per passenger mile are also associated with stronger financial performance as measured by the revenue/cost ratio but not by the net loss per passenger mile.

The analysis also contains a somewhat troubling finding. Amtrak's financial performance, as indicated by the measures used in this analysis, is better when its locomotive fleet is older. A significant proportion of the improvement in Amtrak's financial performance in the 1980s apparently was due to the virtual absence of investment in new equipment. The phenomenon of limited investment is not unique to the Amtrak system, however. A number of studies have commented recently on the limited public-sector investment in all sorts of infrastructure, from highways and railroads to water mains and sewage treatment plants.[28] Postponing major renovation and modernization of facilities can produce short-run savings but brings the risk of deterioration of those facilities in the long run.

That concern clearly is relevant for the Amtrak system. As the average age of locomotives rose from seven years in 1985 to eleven in 1989, the percentage of locomotives not available for service on an average day rose from 6.8 percent to 13.0 percent. In addition, the percentage of long distance trains that were on time fell from 78 percent to 54 percent.[29] Many factors influence the on-time performance of long distance trains: the condition of equipment, weather, and the cooperativeness of the railroads that own the track, among other things. Nevertheless, the steady increase in the age of the locomotive fleet in the late 1980s and the steady decline of on-time performance are cause for concern. Here, as in other aspects of the nation's infrastructure, neglected investment eventually brings costs of one form or another.

Finally, the preceding analysis indirectly confirms the validity of Amtrak's efforts to improve the appeal of passenger train service. These efforts have taken many forms, from improvements in food quality and on-board movies to aggressive advertising, route modifications, and coordinated bus service.[30] The results have been striking: total passenger miles rose from 3.04 billion to 6.27 billion in 1991, and passenger miles per train mile rose from 117 in 1972 to 188 in 1989, followed by a slight decline.[31] By increasing passenger volume, these efforts have helped improve the system's financial performance.

Notes

1. For examples, see *Improving Productivity in State and Local Government* (New York: Committee for Economic Development, 1976); William Martin, *Motivation and Productivity in Public Sector Human Organizations* (New York: Quorum, 1988); Elaine Morley, *A Practitioner's Guide to Public Sector Productivity Improvement* (New York: Van Nostrand Reinhold, 1986).

2. George Downs and Patrick Larkey, *The Quest for Government Efficiency* (Philadelphia: Temple University Press, 1986).

3. Walter Balk, *Improving Government Productivity* (Beverly Hills: Sage, 1975), 5; Barry Bozeman, *Public Management and Policy Analysis* (New York: St. Martin's, 1979), 359; Downs and Larkey, 9–11; Peter Drucker, *Management* (New York: Harper and Row, 1973), 67–68, 111; Nancy Hayward and George Kuper, "The National Economy and Productivity in Government," *Public Administration Review* 38 (1978): 2; Morley, 3.

4. Balk, 7–12; Downs and Larkey, 6–8; Harry Hatry, "The Status of Productivity Measurement in the Public Sector," *Public Administration Review* 38 (1978): 28; Robert Pursely and Neil Snortland, *Managing Government Organizations* (North Scituate, MA: Duxbury, 1980), 442.

5. *Improving Productivity*, 15–16; Pursely and Snortland, 453–454.

6. Drucker, 29, 68–71, 112–113.

7. See *Federal Subsidies for Rail Passenger Service*: *An Assessment of Amtrak* (Washington, DC: Congressional Budget Office, 1982); Francis Mulvey, "Amtrak: A Cost-Effectiveness Analysis," *Transportation Research* 13A (1979): 329–344.

8. *Annual Report* (Washington, DC: National Railroad Passenger Corporation, 1988), 3–4; *Annual Report* (Washington, DC: National Railroad Passenger Corporation, 1994), 8–10, 19–27.

9. Robert Bish and Vincent Ostrom, *Understanding Urban Government* (Washington, DC: American Enterprise Institute, 1973), 29–31; Harold Gortner, *Administration in the Public Sector*, 2nd ed. (New York: Wiley, 1981), 149; *Improving Productivity*, 22, 61–62.

10. Martin Farris and Forrest Harding, *Passenger Transportation* (Englewood Cliffs, NJ: Prentice-Hall, 1976), 71.

11. Harold Gortner, Julianne Mahler, and Jeanne Nicholson, *Organization Theory* (Chicago: Dorsey, 1987), 30.

12. See Chapter 2; see also David Nice, "Stability of the Amtrak System," *Transportation Quarterly* 43 (1989): 566–568.

13. For overviews, see Downs and Larkey, chs. 4, 6; Martin, chs. 4–10; Morley, chs. 8–13.

14. John Stover, *The Life and Decline of the American Railroad* (New York: Oxford, 1970), 218.

15. George Hilton, *Amtrak* (Washington, DC: American Enterprise Institute, 1980), 39–42.

16. Downs and Larkey, 246–251; Harry Hatry, "Current State of the Art of State and Local Government Productivity Improvement—and Potential Federal Roles," in *Managing Fiscal Stress,* ed. Charles Levine (Chatham, NJ: Chatham House, 1980), 272–273; Hayward and Kuper, 3.

17. Paul Peterson, Barry Rabe, and Kenneth Wong, *When Federalism Works* (Washington, DC: Brookings, 1986), 131–132, 158–174.

18. Rodger Bradley, *Amtrak* (Poole, United Kingdom: Blandford Press, 1985), 64–116; Patrick Dorin, *Amtrak Trains and Travel* (Seattle: Superior, 1979), 15, 18, 24–27; Nice; "Stability"; Karl Zimmerman, *Amtrak at Milepost 10* (Park Forest, IL: PTJ Publishing, 1981), 3–7, 39, 74.

19. Farris and Harding, 71–72.

20. Hilton, 36–37.

21. Bish and Ostrom, 10, 75–78; Gortner, 29; Duncan MacRae and James Wilde, *Policy Analysis for Public Decisions* (North Scituate, MA: Duxbury, 1979), 165, 176.

22. Donald Harper, *Transportation in America,* 2nd ed. (Englewood Cliffs, NJ: Prentice-Hall, 1982), 220–222.

23. MacRae and Wilde, 176.

24. Bish and Ostrom, 78.

25. *Annual Report* (Washington, DC: National Railroad Passenger Corporation, 1989), 2, 7.

26. See, for example, *Annual Report* (1988), 4–5.

27. See Downs and Larkey for an overview of that phenomenon.

28. Robert Berne and Richard Schramm, *The Financial Analysis of Governments* (Englewood Cliffs, NJ: Prentice-Hall, 1986), 169–173; Pat Choate and Susan Walter, *America in Ruins* (Durham, NC: Duke, 1981), 1–4, 30–33; *Public Works Infrastructure: Policy Considerations for the 1980s* (Washington, DC: Advisory Commission on Intergovernmental Relations, 1983), 1–8; Simon Webley, *Stiffening the Sinews of the Nations* (London: British–North American Committee, 1985), 18–32.

29. *Annual Report* (1989), 21.

30. *Annual Report* (1989), 12–15; *Annual Report* (Washington, DC: National Railroad Passenger Corporation, 1986), 9, 17, 19.

31. See *Annual Report* (1989); Bradley, 123; *Statistical Appendix to Amtrak FY 1994 Annual Report* (Washington, DC: National Railroad Passenger Corporation, 1994).

8

Amtrak: Worth the Cost?

Throughout U.S. history, the public sector has been involved actively in shaping the development and operation of the transportation system, although private decisions also have played a major role. Moreover, governmental involvement in the transportation field is not limited to the United States; governments around the world are active participants in their transportation systems.

Many aspects of public involvement in transportation are relatively noncontroversial. Public funding for road and highway programs is widely accepted at the national, state, and local levels, although disagreements arise from time to time over the distribution of funds, contract awards, and location of new routes. Public ownership of major airports is widely accepted in principle, as is public involvement in the air traffic control system. Governmental programs to improve harbors and waterways generate occasional criticism but rarely face serious attack.

A major exception, although not the only one, to the consensual nature of transportation programs is the Amtrak system, which has been embroiled in controversy for much of its existence. A major element of the controversy regarding Amtrak centers on the question of whether it produces benefits that are sufficient to justify its costs. Policy and performance assessment of Amtrak involves numerous complexities, as we have seen, but certain tentative conclusions have been possible. Beyond assessments based on Amtrak's own record, however, an evaluation might also place that record in the context of broader national issues.

Energy

One aspect of the Amtrak controversy involves its potential contribution to U.S. energy independence. The U.S. transportation system is powered almost entirely by oil. It accounts for approximately two-thirds of all U.S.

oil consumption,[1] contributing over time to a substantial decline in U.S. petroleum reserves and to heavy dependence on imported oil. Proven U.S. petroleum reserves declined virtually every year from 1976 through 1992, with a decline of roughly 20 percent from 1980 through 1992.[2] Petroleum imports have risen considerably since the mid-1980s, and imports of oil from OPEC countries have increased especially rapidly. By 1994, OPEC accounted for over half of all U.S. oil imports.[3] Oil imports as a percentage of U.S. oil consumption have been increasing for a number of years; by 1993, imports virtually equalled domestic oil production.[4]

The enormous petroleum requirements of the U.S. transportation system have been a source of concern to many observers. At current rates of production and discovery, known U.S. petroleum reserves are likely to become rather skimpy within the next twenty to thirty years; additional deposits will be found, but the bulk of the readily recoverable reserves probably has been discovered. Moreover, approximately two-thirds of the world's known oil reserves are located in the OPEC countries, many of which have alternated between high levels of instability and outright warfare since World War II.[5]

The transportation system's heavy dependence on imported oil has contributed to the nation's balance of payments deficit. In the event of a major disruption in the flow of imports, this extensive dependence would also produce serious disruptions in the system, although modest interruptions could be absorbed without great difficulty.[6] Moreover, although long-term projections are not always dependable, recent patterns of consumption, dependence, and availability of reserves suggest strongly that the system will grow increasingly dependent on imported oil, a situation that will heighten the nation's vulnerability to supply interruptions and balance of payments problems. Not surprisingly, then, a number of observers contend that the nation needs to reduce its reliance on petroleum and make greater use of other energy sources.[7]

Passenger trains sometimes have been depicted as part of the solution to the nation's petroleum problems. With high energy efficiency, at least with high traffic loads, passenger trains can provide mobility for the public while reducing oil consumption. As a result, domestic oil supplies can be conserved and imports reduced.

Critics of this perspective contend that the amount of petroleum saved by Amtrak is comparatively small and that other strategies, such as lower highway speeds, improved automobile fuel economy, and synthetic fuels projects, would be more cost-effective. These critics also note that the Amtrak system is too small to handle more than a small fraction of the nation's highway and air traffic in the event of a crisis.[8]

There is little doubt that there are many ways to reduce the nation's oil consumption. Strategies that directly encourage conservation are likely to have greater short-term impact than is the Amtrak system. However, a number of programs designed to encourage energy conservation have been repealed in the last fifteen years, and funding for synthetic fuels development has been slashed.[9] Speed limits on many highways have been raised, and higher speeds mean more fuel consumption. Policies that have technical merit but are unable to survive in the political arena will contribute little to energy independence, even in the short run.

Moreover, the capital-intensive nature of the transportation system calls for consideration of long-term needs as well as short-term effects. The first national legislation to create the Interstate Highway System was passed in the 1940s, but the system was not substantially complete until approximately 1980. A new airport or mass transit system takes years to complete. Fundamental changes in system capability, then, must be evaluated in light of future as well as contemporary circumstances.

Transportation analysts long have known that electrified rail systems can carry large volumes of passengers and freight without using oil for propulsion.[10] With current patterns of transportation use, the resulting reduction in oil consumption would be comparatively small.[11] However, a sustained program of capacity building and incentives for construction and use of electrified rail transportation could yield petroleum savings that are larger than current transportation patterns indicate.[12] In addition, a major crisis unquestionably would trigger a major curtailment of nonessential transportation use, both for passenger travel and freight movements. Capabilities that appear modest when compared to the total transportation load, then, may seem more substantial when compared to essential transportation activities.

The benefits of a large-scale rail electrification program (involving the 20,000 most heavily used miles of the rail system) would emerge slowly, for the program probably would take roughly twenty years to complete.[13] Most of Amtrak's busy Northeast Corridor is already electrified, and steps are being taken to extend electrification east from New Haven to Boston. Large-scale electrification is not a policy option that can produce immediate relief if begun after a major supply disruption is already underway, but it is a policy option with possible benefits for both freight and passenger transportation—an option already in use in a number of other countries.

Efforts to develop a new generation of coal-powered locomotives may provide another method for promoting energy independence on the railroads.[14] The United States has enormous reserves of coal, and conversion to coal-powered locomotives would not require as large a capital investment as would rail electrification. The annual projected cost of electrification over a period of twenty years is not staggering, but the total cost is somewhat daunting, especially in an era of national budget deficits and low railroad profitability.[15] Coal-powered locomotives, furthermore, could operate on virtually all railroad lines, assuming that fueling stations are located suitably. Electric locomotives, in contrast, can be used only on electrified routes, a circumstance that limits their operating flexibility.

The key advantage of electrification, however, is its proven capacity to handle high volumes of traffic in an environmentally sound fashion. The environmental and energy benefits of electrified rail transportation depend on how the electricity is generated. If and when successful fusion reactors are developed, enormous supplies of electricity can be generated with little environmental harm. Coal-fired generators present problems of emissions that contribute to acid rain and the greenhouse effect, among other things. Whether a new type of coal-powered locomotive can function with acceptable environmental costs remains uncertain at this point.

Viewed in long-term perspective, the Amtrak system emerges as part of a broader strategy to reduce the transportation system's enormous appetite for oil. Evaluations of future benefits are always clouded by substantial uncertainty, since projections of future patterns of transportation demand, energy availability, and other relevant considerations inevitably are imprecise. Given that creation of basic transportation systems takes years, however, analysts cannot afford to ignore future conditions; the relatively negative evaluations of Amtrak all share a short-term focus that overlooks longer-term considerations.

The precise magnitude of Amtrak's potential contribution to the reduction of oil consumption depends on a number of uncertain factors. Whether the main railroad lines are electrified, for example, or whether incentives such as higher motor fuel taxes are adopted, bear directly on the outcome. Broadly speaking, the nation has shown little willingness to reduce the transportation system's appetite for oil since 1981, whether we consider governmental actions (raising speed limits, for example) or private sector decisions, such as the types of vehicles consumers buy.

Service Quality

The quality of Amtrak's service received significant criticism in its early years. On-time performance often was poor,[16] in large measure because of the poor condition of Amtrak's equipment when operations began. Traveling by Amtrak proved to be slower than traveling by other modes on many routes, and schedules and station locations in some localities were relatively inconvenient.[17]

Improving service quality has been a major concern of Amtrak's management from the beginning. Deliveries of new equipment and rebuilding older equipment helped to improve passenger comfort and on-time performance by the early 1980s, but adherence to schedules slumped in the mid-1980s, generally the result of overused equipment, the aging of the locomotive fleet, and lengthened maintenance cycles.[18] Travel times have improved for some trips, largely because of route changes and track improvements in the Northeast Corridor.[19] On-board telephone service has been added on some trains, and the ticketing and reservation system has been made faster and more convenient. Movies, route guides, and other amenities have been added to long-distance trains. Station improvements have been undertaken in numerous localities, the most dramatic example being the renovation of Union Station in Washington, D.C.[20]

Other efforts to improve service are underway. New passenger cars have been acquired recently, and others are now on order. The development of new Viewliner equipment will permit replacement of the aging Heritage Fleet, which is the mainstay of long-distance trains in the eastern part of the country and has remained in service beyond its normal operating life. The Viewliner cars will offer many improvements, including more efficient climate control systems, windows for passengers in the upper berths of sleeping cars, and lower maintenance costs.[21] Much-needed new locomotives are also going into service, including a new generation of high-horsepower diesels for some long-distance trains.

Route improvements, another important aspect of service quality, have been limited in recent years by budgetary constraints, but some improvements have been adopted. The institution of direct service from Santa Barbara, California, to San Diego eliminated a change of trains in Los Angeles and has attracted substantial ridership. Construction of the West Side Connection permits through train service between the former New York Central route north of New York City and Pennsylvania Station, with its connections to the east, west, and south. The connection permits direct service between major points on Amtrak's Empire Corridor, points such as Albany, Buffalo, and Toronto, and major Northeast Corridor terminals, such as Baltimore, Philadelphia, and Washington, D.C. Travel between those corridors traditionally has required not only a change of trains but a change of stations as well. On the less positive side, budgetary constraints in the mid-1990s resulted in the termination of the Broadway Limited, which provided service to New York City, Philadelphia, Pittsburgh, and Chicago, as well as termination of two western trains, the Desert Wind and the Pioneer.[22]

Overall, the record indicates a substantial number of improvements in service quality and an ongoing effort to achieve further improvements. Not coincidentally, passenger volume (measured in passenger miles) has risen considerably over the course of Amtrak's existence. As suggested by the discouragement hypothesis, a management team committed to attracting passengers has been able to do just that.

Perhaps the most dramatic prospect for future service quality improvements is magnetic levitation technology, which transports trains on a magnetic field instead of wheels. This technology, which is now being tested in Japan and Germany, offers the possibility of speeds of 250 miles per hour or more and a virtually bumpless ride.[23] At that speed, a passenger train could travel from Boston to New York in approximately one hour.

Whether the technology will ever prove feasible for large-scale use remains to be seen, but if it is successful, it would expand greatly the range of routes for which trains could compete with air travel for time-conscious travelers.

Economic Considerations

Critics of Amtrak have charged that it receives disproportionately high subsidies in comparison with other transportation modes relative to the number of passengers served. The high subsidies are an outgrowth, at least in part, of Amtrak's disproportionately high costs. The critics generally conclude that the resources used to sustain the Amtrak system would be more productive if used for other purposes.[24]

The disproportionate subsidy criticism suffers from two basic problems. First, the most widely cited study examines only direct, national government subsidies to our major transportation systems. In the case of Amtrak, that captures all the subsidies it receives except for a small contribution from state subsidy programs. In the cases of road and air transportation, however, examining only direct national subsidies omits a great deal.[25]

Most road and highway expenditures are made by state and local governments, and a substantial proportion of these outlays, especially at the local level, is a net subsidy. A study published by the U.S. Department of Transportation concluded that 39 percent of all U.S. highway expenditures in 1981 were not from user fees. Seventeen percent of all state spending and fully 93 percent of all local spending for roads and highways did not come from user fees and were, therefore, net subsidies.[26] Omitting state and local activities, then, omits most of the direct highway subsidies.

In addition, road and highway programs benefit from a wide variety of indirect subsidies that are omitted from most discussions of the issue. The interest costs of automobile purchases were deductible from federal income taxes for many years, and with the home equity loan provision the same subsidy is still available for homeowners. The substantial law enforcement costs generated by road-based transportation are largely funded from general revenues. The disproportionately high accident rates of automobile travel[27] generate costs that are shifted to nonusers through a host of general mechanisms for sharing risks: life insurance, disability income programs, Social Security, and the like. Uninsured motorists—by some estimates, possibly 15 to 20 percent of all motorists—also shift the costs of their accidents to private and public health insurance programs and to hospitals, which in turn shift the costs of unpaid bills to their owners and/or other customers. Policies that subsidize the oil industry, such as the oil depletion allowance, also indirectly aid petroleum-powered cars. According to some estimates, the oil depletion allowance in the late 1960s cost the U.S. Treasury approximately $7 billion per year.[28]

Air transportation also benefits from a variety of subsidies, both direct and indirect. The nation's larger airports are publicly owned, as are many smaller facilities. According to one estimate, the annual loss of market-based rent, including property taxes, from publicly owned airports in the United States was roughly $750 million by the late 1970s.[29] This sum is almost identical to the amount of money lost by the railroads on private passenger service in 1957, the worst year on record.[30]

Furthermore, much of the technology used in modern aircraft design, navigation, and traffic control was developed from government-sponsored research. For example, federal subsidies for jet aircraft engine research in fiscal year 1988 reached $1.02 billion (not counting funds in the so-called black budget for more secret programs), a sum that was nearly double the federal subsidy for the entire Amtrak system that year.[31] While this research was for military aircraft, many of its results undoubtedly will find their way into civilian aircraft design, as has happened in the past.

Other indirect subsidies of air travel lie in the deduction of business travel expenses from taxable corporate income. In addition, many airline pilots, navigators, and other personnel received much of their initial training from the U.S. Department of Defense, which not only bore the cost of their training but also sifted out individuals who appeared to be qualified but could not perform adequately. The latter service reduces the uncertainty costs borne by the airlines. Moreover, previous subsidies of local air service and regulations that limited competition on longer flights (prior to deregulation) added to airline coffers.

Comparisons of subsidies given to various transportation modes in the late 1970s or early 1980s also are suspect unless the historical context is taken into account. As noted in Chapter 2, some of Amtrak's largest expenditures, involving modernization of its equipment, ticketing system, and work rules, were needed to compensate for the major decline in investment in passenger trains during the fifteen years prior to Amtrak's creation. There is no doubt that Amtrak has struggled to correct for past neglect in a variety of respects. In this light, given the sustained flow of subsidies to road transportation systems for most of this century and to the airlines for approximately half a century, the charge that Amtrak receives disproportionately high subsidies is of uncertain validity.

Clearly, Amtrak's reliance on subsidies has declined in recent years. Federal operating subsidies declined by 45 percent from 1985 to 1994. Amtrak's ratio of revenues (excluding subsidies) to expenses rose from .37 in 1978 to .80 in 1993, then declined slightly to .77 in 1994.[32] Mulvey's projection that Amtrak's annual losses would reach $1.72 billion by 1990 proved to be overly pessimistic; the actual loss that year was 59 percent lower.[33] By a variety of indicators, financial performance has improved considerably, as would be expected in any organization that begins with a burden of past neglect and must devote substantial effort and resources to compensating for that neglect. Further progress on productivity clearly is desirable; according to one analysis, Amtrak's total costs per passenger mile in 1986 were approximately 33¢—somewhat lower than the cost per vehicle mile of a large sedan in its first year of operation but higher than the cost per vehicle mile of any car averaged over twelve years of ownership.[34]

National Security

Analysts long have known that a sound and dependable transportation system is vital to national security. If a nation's transportation system cannot move large numbers of people and large quantities of materials for extended periods, substantial conventional military efforts will be extremely difficult to sustain. Moreover, a common military tactic involves targeting vulnerable components of a transportation system in order to interrupt movements of personnel and supplies. The ability of the transportation system to cope with large traffic volume under adverse conditions is therefore a key component of national security.[35]

From the Civil War to the present, railroads in the United States have played a major role in meeting the transportation needs of military mobilizations. That role is partially an outgrowth of the railroads' ability to handle heavy traffic volume with comparatively modest resources.[36] The Amtrak system too, some observers believe, could play a significant role in future military emergencies, both in handling movements of military personnel and, perhaps more importantly, in facilitating civilian mobility.[37]

Critics of this point of view note that the national security role of trains has been reduced by the development of highway and air travel systems.[38] Aircraft can move vital military supplies and personnel much more rapidly than can trains, and the highway system, although slower than air travel, can handle immense traffic volume. Moreover, the disintegration of the Soviet Union has led many people to believe that national security problems generally will be less serious in future years.

The national security benefits of the Amtrak system depend, in part, on the breadth of perspective employed as well as the time horizon utilized. If arms negotiations ultimately are successful in reducing the role of strategic nuclear weapons in military relationships, greater emphasis on conventional weapons systems is likely to result. The collapse of communism in the Soviet Union is likely to have the same effect. Protecting national security through conventional weapons systems has several interrelated implications for the domestic transportation system.

First, conventional military conflict can and often does continue for years, in contrast to the comparatively short duration of strategic nuclear war. The transportation system's ability to function through several years of stress becomes increasingly important as reliance on conventional weapons increases. Second, a transportation system that is heavily dependent on imported energy sources, as is the case for the United States, is vulnerable to supply disruptions, particularly if a conflict lasts for an extended period. A simultaneous escalation of military needs for petroleum fuels and difficulty in importing oil could yield great difficulty for this country in a situation of prolonged warfare.

Third, a protracted conventional conflict on a large scale would produce immense demands on military airlift capability. The result would be diversion of much of the nation's airline fleet to military uses. Civilian air travel would be greatly curtailed, both by the lack of available aircraft and by the military's aviation fuel needs.

The Amtrak system could conceivably be part of a broader strategy to develop a passenger and freight transportation network that could function despite a prolonged shortage of oil for civilian transportation uses. As noted earlier, development of an electrified rail system and of coal-powered locomotives would be important in this respect. A gradual expansion of the system, coupled with policies to encourage ridership and conserve petroleum fuels, could yield more substantial capacity for future emergencies. Less dramatically, these approaches could contribute to making U.S. foreign policy generally less vulnerable to the agendas of oil-producing nations.[39]

Of course, other efforts to reduce the vulnerability of the U.S. transportation system are underway. The Strategic Petroleum Reserve gives the nation a stockpile of oil for use in the event of a major disruption in the flow of oil imports. From a national security standpoint, however, the Strategic Petroleum Reserve presents several significant problems. First, by concentrating vast amounts of a vital resource in a very few locations, it presents a dangerously attractive target for sabotage or attack.[40]

Second, current projections for oil consumption and oil imports indicate that the Strategic Petroleum Reserve, in the absence of very strong measures to reduce consumption dramatically, would be exhausted in a few months. Although some studies have concluded that drawing down oil reserves would cause less economic harm than would imposition of measures to restrain demand in the event of a short-term supply disruption,[41] policymakers are unlikely to know how long a supply disruption might last. If the disruption lasts longer than expected, the draw-down strategy risks exhaustion of reserves while making no preparation for dealing with a longer-lasting disruption.

Efficiency Concerns, Narrowly Defined

The analyses presented in preceding chapters indicate that, contrary to the expectations of critics, Amtrak policies and performance records demonstrate significant concern with efficiency. First, the national distribution of

Amtrak service is substantially consistent with measures of market potential. Although political influences have played some role in the distribution of service over the years, those considerations have modest impact when compared with the influence of probable traffic volume. Second, analysis of state subsidy programs reveals that, in general, states in which passenger rail services is unlikely to be economical are unlikely to adopt subsidies and, if they do adopt them, are unlikely to retain them. Third, Amtrak's decisions regarding international rail services have clearly been consistent with measures of traffic potential. Here, as in the case of state subsidies, we see a willingness to reconsider service based on experience.

Finally, contrary to the expectations of many observers, Amtrak has demonstrated significant progress in winning back the public's interest in passenger train travel, and the increasing ridership has of course helped to improve the financial performance of the system. Problems remain, however, in the lack of consistent funding for capital investment; those problems can be resolved only by Congress and the White House.

Conclusions

A basic investment strategy holds that, in times of uncertainty, investors should diversify their holdings rather than put all their assets into one company's stock. The U.S. transportation system reflects a striking rejection of that advice: the system is powered almost entirely by a single energy source, oil. Although the 1973 oil embargo and the 1979–1980 embargo gave dramatic demonstrations of the risks of the system's near-total reliance on oil, much of it imported, the United States generally has been unable to establish and maintain a coherent strategy to cope with the problem.[42] Conservation incentives have been adopted and repealed; speed limits have been lowered and then raised. Part of the difficulty facing transportation policy analysts is in fashioning a package of proposals that combine short- and long-run benefits as well as political feasibility.

In view of the instability of many energy-related programs in the past two decades, the survival of the Amtrak system seems a noteworthy achievement. No prudent observer, of course, would advocate viewing Amtrak as the only strategy for promoting energy independence or national security. We do know that, in the long run, railroads have the proven ability to move passengers and freight without oil-based fuels. Future conditions are far from certain, but waiting until the uncertainty is eliminated risks leaving the nation seriously unprepared and vulnerable.[43]

The United States is a large and complex nation with many transportation needs. We do not seem to be unduly alarmed at the prospect of spending $1 billion in a single year on jet aircraft engine research, $140 million for a single mile of urban expressway, or more than $10 billion for an expressway project for a single metropolitan area.[44] Available information on America's oil reserves and oil consumption suggests, however, that at least modest investment in transportation modes that can be more readily converted to operation without oil fuels may well be prudent. The Amtrak system meets that requirement.

The preceding analysis also indicates that public or quasi-public agencies are capable of improving their performance. The early Amtrak system suffered from the neglect of passenger train service in its waning years in the private sector and from strikingly diverse expectations regarding its goals. With time, effort, and money came new equipment, improved facilities, and modernized work rules. Many characteristics of the system, from the national distribution of service and state subsidy programs to the evolution of international service and the system's financial performance, reflect efforts to allocate resources productively and to control costs. Not all public agencies operate in an environment featuring as much competition as does Amtrak, but the evidence presented here demonstrates that concern for efficiency is not a stranger to the public sector.

Notes

1. *Energy Security: An Overview of Changes in the World Oil Market* (Washington, DC: General Accounting Office, 1988), 20.

2. *U.S. Crude Oil, Natural Gas, and Natural Gas Liquids Reserves: 1986 Annual Report* (Washington, DC: Energy Information Administration, 1987), 6; *American Almanac* (Austin, TX: Reference Press, 1994), 717.

3. *World Almanac* (New York: Newspaper Enterprise Association, 1988), 175; (1990), 191; (1996), 202.

4. *Energy Security*, 24; *American Almanac*, 583–584, 594.

5. *Energy Security*, 39–43; *World Almanac* (New York: Newspaper Enterprise Association, 1991), 192.

6. For a troubling assessment of the state of U.S. emergency reserves, see *International Energy Agency* (Washington, DC: General Accounting Office, 1989).

7. Ronald Inglehart, "Value Change in Industrial Societies," *American Political Science Review* 81 (1987): 1302.

8. *Federal Subsidies for Rail Passenger Service: An Assessment of Amtrak* (Washington, DC: Congressional Budget Office, 1982), 13–18; Francis Mulvey, "Amtrak: A Cost-Effectiveness Analysis," *Transportation Research* 13A (1979): 331–333.

9. Don Cash and Robert Rycroft, "Energy Policy: How Failure Was Snatched from the Jaws of Success," *Policy Studies Review* 4 (1985): 433–444; Thomas Dye, *Understanding Public Policy*, 5th ed. (Englewood Cliffs, NJ: Prentice-Hall, 1984), 191.

10. Liviu Alston, *Railways and Energy* (Washington, DC: World Bank, 1984); *Railroad Electrification: The Issues*, Special Report 180 (Washington, DC: National Academy of Science, 1977).

11. Alston, 35.

12. Cecil Law, "Comment," in *Railroad Electrification: The Issues*, 64–65.

13. Law, 64–65.

14. "Coal-Fueled Power: An Assist from DOE," *Railway Age* (December 1986): 24.

15. Alston, 22–24; Richard Fishbein, "Financial Considerations of Railroad Electrification," in *Railroad Electrification: The Issues*, 16.

16. *Report to the President and Congress: Effectiveness of the Act: Amtrak* (Washington, DC: Interstate Commerce Commission, 1979), 7–8.

17. Mulvey, 335–336; Karl Zimmerman, *Amtrak at Milepost 10* (Park Forest, IL: PTJ Publishing, 1981), 4–5.

18. Rodger Bradley, *Amtrak* (Poole, United Kingdom: Blandford, 1985), 123; *Annual Report* (Washington, DC: National Railroad Passenger Corporation, 1987), 20; (1988), 4–5; (1994).

19. David Nice, "Changing Program Performance: The Case of Amtrak," *Transportation Journal* 27 (1987), 44–46.

20. *Annual Report* (Washington, DC: National Railroad Passenger Corporation, 1986), 9, 17, 19; (1987), 4.

21. Tom Nelligan, "The Viewliner Venture," *Passenger Train Journal* 123 (1988): 16–22; Frank Wilner, *The Amtrak Story* (Omaha: Simmons-Boardman, 1994), 74.

22. *Annual Report* (Washington, DC: National Railroad Passenger Corporation, 1990); (1994).

23. Frank Malone, "High-Speed Rail: The Economics Behind the Dream," *Railway Age* (April 1986): 42–52; *U.S. Passenger Rail Technologies* (Washington, DC: Office of Technology Assessment, 1983).

24. *Federal Subsidies*; Mulvey.

25. *Federal Subsidies*.

26. N. Kent Bramlett, *The Evolution of the Highway User Charge Principle* (Washington, DC: Federal Highway Administration, 1982), 23; see also Theodore Keeler, *Railroads, Freight, and Public Policy* (Washington, DC: Brookings, 1983), 116–120.

27. George Hilton, *Amtrak* (Washington, DC: American Enterprise Institute, 1980), 53–54.

28. David Davis, *Energy Politics*, 3rd ed. (New York: St. Martin's, 1982), 85.

29. Robert Piper, "Aviation's Hidden Subsidy," *Transportation Quarterly* 29 (1975): 457–475.

30. Figures on annual losses are found in Hilton, 3–4.

31. *Research and Development: Funding of Jet Aircraft Engines for Fiscal Year 1984–1988* (Washington, DC: General Accounting Office, 1989), 1.

32. *Annual Report* (1987); (1990), 1; Bradley, 123, 133; *Statistical Appendix to Amtrak FY 1994 Annual Report* (Washington, DC: National Railroad Passenger Corporation, 1994).

33. Mulvey, 338–339; *Statistical Appendix*.

34. *Annual Report* (1986); *Statistical Abstract* (Washington, DC: Bureau of the Census, 1987), 593. The automobile costs do not include any indirect subsidies, such as the cost of local roads not covered by user-based taxes.

35. Wilson Clark and Jake Page, *Energy, Vulnerability, and War* (New York: Norton, 1981), chapter 1; George Harmon, *Transportation: The Nation's Lifelines* (Washington, DC: Industrial College of the Armed Forces, 1968), 2–3.

36. Harmon, 16.

37. *Federal Subsidies*, 19.

38. *Federal Subsidies*, 17–19.

39. Zachary Smith, "Review of Martin Melosi's *Coping with Abundance: Energy and Environment in Industrial America*," *Social Science Quarterly* 67 (1986): 461–462.

40. Clark and Page, 108.

41. *International Energy*, 17–21, 40–42.

42. Dye, 184–192.

43. *Energy Security*, 70.

44. These cost figures are from John Anderson, "Central Artery/Tunnel Project: Cost and Financing," Testimony Before the Joint Committee on Transportation, The Commonwealth of Massachusetts (Washington, DC: General Accounting Office, 1996); John Due, "Amtrak and State Supported Passenger Trains," *Illinois Business Review* (Summer 1996): 4–7; *Research and Development*.

Bibliography

Adrian, Charles. 1976. *State and Local Governments*, 4th ed. New York: McGraw-Hill.

Adrian, Charles, and Charles Press. 1977. *Governing Urban America*, 5th ed. New York: McGraw-Hill.

Allen, Benjamin, and David Vellenga. 1983. "Public Financing of Railroads Under the New Federalism: The Progress and Problems of Selected Programs." *Transportation Journal* 23: 5–19.

Alston, Liviu. 1984. *Railways and Energy*. Washington, DC: World Bank.

American Almanac. 1994. Austin, TX: Reference Press.

Amtrak: *Cost of Amtrak Railroad Operations*. 1986. Washington, DC: General Accounting Office.

Amtrak National Train Timetables. Periodic. Washington, DC: National Railroad Passenger Corporation.

"Amtrak Ridership Update." 1990. *Passenger Train Journal* 152: 16.

Amtrak Sourcebook. 1988. Washington, DC: National Railroad Passenger Corporation.

Amtrak's Northeast Corridor Trains Operate with a One-Person Locomotive Crew. 1985. Washington, DC: General Accounting Office.

Anagnoson, Theodore. 1982. "Federal Grant Agencies and Congressional Election Campaigns." *American Journal of Political Science* 26: 547–561.

Anderson, James. 1984. *Public Policy-Making*, 3rd ed. New York: Holt, Rinehart, and Winston.

Anderson, John. 1996. *Central Artery/Tunnel Project*: *Cost and Financing*. Testimony Before the Joint Committee on Transportation, Commonwealth of Massachusetts. Washington, DC: General Accounting Office.

Annual Report. Annual. Washington, DC: National Railroad Passenger Corporation.

Army Deployment: *Better Transportation Planning Is Needed*. 1987. Washington, DC: General Accounting Office.

Arnold, R. Douglas. 1979. *Congress and the Bureaucracy*. New Haven: Yale.

Balk, Walter. 1975. *Improving Government Productivity*. Beverly Hills: Sage.

Beebe, Lucius. 1961. *Mixed Train Daily*, 4th ed. Berkeley: Howell-North.

Beebe, Lucius, and Charles Clegg. 1966. *The Trains We Rode*. Berkeley: Howell-North.

Beesley, M. E. 1970. "The Value of Time Spent in Travelling: Some New Evidence." In *The Demand for Travel*: *Theory and Measurement,* edited by Richard Quandt. Lexington, MA: Heath Lexington Books, 221–234.

Berne, Robert, and Richard Schramm. 1986. *The Financial Analysis of Governments.* Englewood Cliffs, NJ: Prentice-Hall.

Berry, Frances, and William Berry. 1990. "State Lottery Adoptions as Policy Innovations: An Event History Analysis." *American Political Science Review* 84: 395–416.

Bibby, John, Cornelius Cotter, James Gibson, and Robert Huckshorn. 1983. "Parties in State Politics." In *Politics in the American States,* 4th ed., edited by Virginia Gray, Herbert Jacob, and Kenneth Vines. Boston: Little, Brown, 59–96.

Bish, Robert, and Vincent Ostrom. 1973. *Understanding Urban Government.* Washington, DC: American Enterprise Institute.

Black, William. 1986. *Railroads for Rent.* Bloomington: Indiana University.

Black, William, and James Runke. 1975. *The States and Rural Rail Preservation.* Lexington, KY: Council of State Governments.

Blalock, Hubert. 1979. *Social Statistics,* rev. 2nd ed. New York: McGraw-Hill.

Bohi, Charles. 1989. "Toasting the Montrealer." *Passenger Train Journal* 141: 8–11.

Bolotin, Frederick, and David Cingranelli. 1983. "Equity and Urban Policy: The Underclass Hypothesis Revisited." *Journal of Politics* 45: 209–219.

Book of the States. 1984. Lexington, KY: Council of State Governments.

Boyle, John, and David Jacobs. 1982. "The Intracity Distribution of Services: A Multivariate Analysis." *American Political Science Review* 76: 371–379.

Bozeman, Barry. 1979. *Public Management and Policy Analysis.* New York: St. Martin's.

Bradley, Roger. 1985. *Amtrak.* Poole, United Kingdom: Blandford.

Bramlett, N. Kent. 1982. *The Evolution of the Highway User Charge Principle.* Washington, DC: Federal Highway Administration.

Break, George. 1980. *Financing Government in a Federal System.* Washington, DC: Brookings.

Brownson, Charles. 1985. *Congressional Staff Directory.* Mount Vernon, VA: Congressional Staff Directory.

Cash, Don, and Robert Rycroft. 1985. "Energy Policy: How Failure Was Snatched from the Jaws of Success." *Policy Studies Review* 4: 433–444.

Choate, Pat, and Susan Walter. 1981. *America in Ruins.* Durham, NC: Duke.

Clark, Wilson, and Jake Page. 1981. *Energy, Vulnerability, and War.* New York: Norton.

"Coal-Fueled Power: An Assist from DOE." 1986. *Railway Age* (December): 24.

Cohen, Jeffrey, and David Nice. 1983. "Changing Party Loyalty of State Delegations to the U.S. House of Representatives." *Western Political Quarterly* 36: 312–325.

Colcord, Frank. 1979. "Urban Transportation and Political Ideology: Sweden and the United States." In *Current Issues in Transportation Policy,* edited by Alan Altshuler. Lexington, MA: Lexington, 3–16.

Congressional Quarterly Almanac. 1972. Washington, DC: Congressional Quarterly.

Congressional Quarterly Weekly Report. 1986. Washington, DC: Congressional Quarterly (January 11), 78–80.

Davidson, Roger, and Walter Oleszek. 1985. *Congress and Its Members,* 2nd ed. Washington, DC: CQ Press.

Davis, David. 1982. *Energy Politics,* 3rd ed. New York: St. Martin's.

Deckard, Barbara. 1976. "Electoral Marginality and Party Loyalty in House Roll Call Voting." *American Journal of Political Science* 20: 469–481.

Derthick, Martha. 1974. *Uncontrollable Spending for Social Services Grants.* Washington, DC: Brookings.

Dilger, Robert. 1983. "Grantsmanship, Formulamanship, and Other Allocational Principles." *Journal of Urban Affairs* 5: 269–286.

Dorin, Patrick. 1979. *Amtrak Trains and Travel*. Seattle: Superior.

Downs, George, and Patrick Larkey. 1986. *The Search for Governmental Efficiency*. Philadelphia: Temple.

Draper, N. R., and H. Smith. 1981. *Applied Regression Analysis*, 2nd ed. New York: Wiley.

Drucker, Peter. 1973. *Management*. New York: Harper and Row.

Drury, George. 1985. *The Historical Guide to North American Railroads*. Milwaukee: Kalmbach.

Due, John. 1996. "Amtrak and State Supported Passenger Trains." *Illinois Business Review* (Summer): 4–7.

———. 1996. "The Evolution of Suburban and Radial Rail Passenger Transportation in the United States." Office of Research Working Paper No. 96-0143. Urbana-Champaign: College of Commerce and Business Administration, University of Illinois.

Dye, Thomas. 1990. *American Federalism: Competition Among Governments*. Lexington, MA: Lexington.

———. 1966. *Politics, Economics, and the Public*. Chicago: Rand McNally.

———. 1981. *Politics in States and Communities*, 4th ed. Englewood Cliffs, NJ: Prentice-Hall.

———. 1988. *Politics in States and Communities*, 6th ed. Englewood Cliffs, NJ: Prentice-Hall.

———. 1984. *Understanding Public Policy*, 5th ed. Englewood Cliffs, NJ.: Prentice-Hall.

Edmonson, Harold. 1972. *Journey to Amtrak*. Milwaukee: Kalmbach.

Edwards, George, and Ira Sharkansky. 1978. *The Policy Predicament*. San Francisco: Freeman.

Energy Security: An Overview of Changes in the World Oil Market. 1988. Washington, D.C.: General Accounting Office.

Farris, Martin, and Forrest Harding. 1976. *Passenger Transportation*. Englewood Cliffs, NJ: Prentice-Hall.

Federal Subsidies for Rail Passenger Service: An Assessment of Amtrak. 1982. Washington, DC: Congressional Budget Office.

Fenno, Richard. 1973. *Congressmen in Committees*. Boston: Little, Brown.

———. 1978. *Home Style*. Boston: Little, Brown.

Ferejohn, John. 1974. *Pork Barrel Politics*. Stanford: Stanford University.

Fiorina, Morris. 1973. "Electoral Margins, Constituency Influence, and Policy Moderation: A Critical Assessment." *American Politics Quarterly* 1: 479–498.

Fishbein, Richard. 1977. "Financial Considerations of Railroad Electrification." In *Railroad Electrification: The Issues*. Washington, DC: National Academy of Science, Special Report 180, 66.

Friedman, Robert. 1990. "The Politics of Transportation." In *Politics in the American States*, 5th ed., edited by Virginia Gray, Herbert Jacob, and Robert Albritton. Glenview, IL: Scott, Foresman/Little, Brown, 527–559.

Gardiner, Paul. 1978. "National Transportation Policy and National Defense: Partners or Apart?" *Proceedings of the Transportation Research Forum* 19: 12–19.

Gortner, Harold. 1981. *Administration in the Public Sector*, 2nd ed. New York: Wiley.

Gortner, Harold, Julianne Mahler, and Jeanne Nicholson. 1987. *Organization Theory*. Chicago: Dorsey.

Harmon, George. 1968. *Transportation: The Nation's Lifelines*. Washington, DC: Industrial College of the Armed Forces.

Harper, Donald. 1982. *Transportation in America*, 2nd ed. Englewood Cliffs, NJ: Prentice-Hall.

Hatry, Harry. 1980. "Current State of the Art of State and Local Government Productivity Improvement—And Potential Federal Roles." In *Managing Fiscal Stress,* edited by Charles Levine. Chatham, NJ: Chatham House, 269–280.

———. 1978. "The Status of Productivity Measurement in the Public Sector." *Public Administration Review* 38: 28–33.

Hayward, Nancy, and George Kuper. 1978. "The National Economy and Productivity in Government." *Public Administration Review* 38: 2–5.

Hilton, George. 1980. *Amtrak.* Washington, DC: American Enterprise Institute.

Hofferbert, Richard, and John Urice. 1985. "Small-Scale Policy: The Federal Stimulus Versus Competing Explanations for State Funding of the Arts." *American Journal of Political Science* 29: 308–329.

Hollingsworth, J. B., and P. B. Whitehouse. 1977. *American Railroads.* London: Bison.

Hubbard, Freeman. 1981. *Encyclopedia of North American Railroading.* New York: McGraw-Hill.

Improving Productivity in State and Local Government. 1976. New York: Committee for Economic Development.

Inglehart, Ronald. 1987. "Value Change in Industrial Societies." *American Political Science Review* 81: 1289–1303.

International Energy Agency. 1989. Washington, DC: General Accounting Office.

Jensen, Oliver. 1975. *American Heritage History of Railroads in America.* New York: Bonanza.

Jones, Bryan. 1981. "Party and Bureaucracy: The Influence of Intermediary Groups on Urban Public Service Delivery." *American Political Science Review* 75: 688–700.

Jones, Charles. 1976. "Regulating the Environment." In *Politics in the American States*, 3rd ed., edited by Herbert Jacob and Kenneth Vines. Boston: Little, Brown, 388–427.

"Journal, The." 1988. *Passenger Train Journal* 19: 4.

"Journal Update." 1991. *Passenger Train Journal* 22: 13.

Kaufman, Herbert. 1976. *Are Government Organizations Immortal?* Washington, DC: Brookings.

Keeler, Theodore. 1983. *Railroads, Freight, and Public Policy.* Washington, DC: Brookings.

Kingdon, John. 1981. *Congressman's Voting Decisions*, 2nd ed. New York: Harper and Row.

Koehler, David, and Margaret Wrightson. 1987. "Inequality in the Delivery of Urban Services: A Reconsideration of Chicago Parks." *Journal of Politics* 49: 80–99.

Kostroski, Warren. 1973. "Party and Incumbency in Postwar Senate Elections: Trends, Patterns, and Models." *American Political Science Review* 67: 1213–1234.

Law, Cecil. 1977. "Comment." In *Railroad Electrification: The Issues*. Washington, DC: National Academy of Science, Special Report 180, 64–65.

Levine, Charles, ed. 1980. *Managing Fiscal Stress.* Chatham, NJ: Chatham House.

Lineberry, Robert. 1978. *American Public Policy.* New York: Harper and Row.

———. 1977. *Equality and Urban Policy.* Beverly Hills: Sage.

Lipsky, Michael. 1980. *Street Level Bureaucracy.* New York: Russell Sage.

Lowi, Theodore. 1979. *The End of Liberalism*, 2nd ed. New York: Norton.

Lyon, Peter. 1968. *To Hell in a Day Coach*. Philadelphia: Lippincott.

MacRae, Duncan, and James Wilde. 1979. *Policy Analysis for Public Decisions*. North Scituate, MA: Duxbury.

Malone, Frank. 1986. "High-Speed Rail: The Economics Behind the Dream." *Railway Age* (April): 42–52.

Mansfield, Edwin. 1983. *Statistics for Business and Economics*, 2nd ed. New York: Norton.

Martin, William. 1988. *Motivation and Productivity in Public Sector Human Organizations*. New York: Quorum.

Masters, Nicholas. 1961. "House Committee Assignments." *American Political Science Review* 55: 345–357.

McGregor, Eugene. 1978. "Uncertainty and National Nominating Coalitions." *Journal of Politics* 40: 1011–1043.

Mladenka, Kenneth. 1980. "The Urban Bureaucracy and the Chicago Political Machine: Who Gets What and the Limits to Political Control." *American Political Science Review* 74: 991–998.

"Money Is Roadblock to Revival of Passenger Trains." 1970. *Congressional Quarterly Weekly Report* 28: 353.

Morgan, David. 1959. "Who Shot the Passenger Train?" *Trains* 19: 14–51.

Morley, Elaine. 1986. *A Practitioner's Guide to Public Sector Productivity Improvement*. New York: Van Nostrand Reinhold.

Morris, Inez, and David Morris. 1977. *North America by Rail*. Indianapolis: Bobbs-Merrill.

Mulvey, Francis. 1979. "Amtrak: A Cost-Effectiveness Analysis." *Transportation Research* 13A: 239–344.

National Transportation Statistics. 1980. Washington, DC: Department of Transportation.

National Transportation Trends and Choices. 1977. Washington, DC: Department of Transportation.

Nelligan, Tom. 1988. "The Viewliner Venture." *Passenger Train Journal* 19 (March): 16–22.

Nelson, James. 1959. *Railroad Transportation and Public Policy*. Washington, DC: Brookings.

"New Railroad Passenger System: Running in the Red." 1971. *Congressional Quarterly Weekly Report* 29: 2622–2626.

"New Service to Mobile." 1996. *Passenger Train Journal* 224: 12–13.

"News Photos." 1987. *Passenger Train Journal* 18: 7.

Nice, David. 1983. "Amtrak in the States." *Policy Studies Journal* 11: 587–597.

———. 1987. "Changing Program Performance: The Case of Amtrak." *Transportation Journal* 27: 43–49.

———. 1989. "Consideration of High-Speed Rail Service in the United States." *Transportation Research* 23A: 359–365.

———. 1994. *Policy Innovation in State Government*. Ames: Iowa State University.

———. 1988. "Program Survival and Termination: State Subsidies of Amtrak." *Transportation Quarterly* 42: 571–585.

———. 1989. "Stability of the Amtrak System." *Transportation Quarterly* 43: 557–570.

———. 1987. "State and Local Government Ownership of Freight Railroads." *Transportation Quarterly* 41: 587–600.

———. 1986. "The States and Amtrak." *Transportation Quarterly* 40: 559–570.

———. 1987. "The States and Passenger Rail Service." *Transportation Research* 21A: 385–390.

Nie, Norman, Sidney Verba, and John Petrocik. 1976. *The Changing American Voter*. Cambridge: Harvard.

Olson, Mancur. 1965. *The Logic of Collective Action*. Cambridge: Harvard.

"On the Property." 1993. *Passenger Train Journal* 189: 24–29.

Palumbo, Dennis. 1988. *Public Policy in America*. San Diego: Harcourt, Brace, Jovanovich.

Peters, B. Guy. 1986. *American Public Policy*, 2nd ed. Chatham, NJ: Chatham House.

Peterson, Paul, Barry Rabe, and Kenneth Wong. 1986. *When Federalism Works*. Washington, DC: Brookings.

Phillips, Don. 1972. "Railpax Rescue." In *Journey to Amtrak*, edited by Harold Edmonson. Milwaukee: Kalmbach, 8–11.

Piper, Robert. 1975. "Aviation's Hidden Subsidy." *Transportation Quarterly* 29: 457–475.

Public Works Infrastructure: Policy Considerations for the 1980s. 1983. Washington, DC: Advisory Commission on Intergovernmental Relations.

Pursely, Robert, and Neil Snortland. 1980. *Managing Government Organizations*. North Scituate, MA: Duxbury.

Quandt, Richard, and William Baumol. 1970. "The Demand for Abstract Transport Modes: Theory and Measurement." In *The Demand for Travel: Theory and Measurement*, edited by Richard Quandt. Lexington, MA: Heath Lexington Books, 83–101.

Railroad Electrification: The Issues. 1977. Washington, DC: National Academy of Science, Special Report 180.

Rand McNally Road Atlas. Annual. Chicago: Rand McNally.

Ranney, Austin. 1976. "Parties in State Politics." In *Politics in the American States*, 3rd ed., edited by Herbert Jacob and Kenneth Vines. Boston: Little, Brown, 51–92.

Report to the President and the Congress: Effectiveness of the Act: Amtrak. 1979. Washington, DC: Interstate Commerce Commission.

Research and Development: Funding of Jet Aircraft Engines for Fiscal Year 1984–1988. 1989. Washington, DC: General Accounting Office.

Ripley, Randall, and Grace Franklin. 1984. *Congress, the Bureaucracy, and Public Policy*, 3rd ed. Homewood, IL: Dorsey.

Rogers, Everett. 1983. *Diffusion of Innovations*, 3rd ed. New York: Free Press.

Rossi, Peter, and Howard Freeman. 1982. *Evaluation*, 2nd ed. Beverly Hills: Sage.

Rourke, Francis. 1984. *Bureaucracy, Politics, and Public Policy*, 3rd ed. Boston: Little, Brown.

Sampson, Roy, Martin Farris, and David Shrock. 1985. *Domestic Transportation*, 5th ed. Boston: Houghton Mifflin.

Sargent, Lyman. 1981. *Contemporary Political Ideologies*, 5th ed. Homewood, IL: Dorsey.

Savage, Robert. 1978. "Policy Innovativeness as a Trait of American States." *Journal of Politics* 40: 212–228.

Schafer, Mike. 1991. *All Aboard Amtrak*. Piscataway, NJ: Railpace.

———. 1991. "Amtrak's Atlas." *Trains* 51: 49–53.

Schiermeyer, Carl, and L. Erik Lange. 1988. "The Making of a Corridor." *Passenger Train Journal* 19: 16–21.

Shaffer, William. 1980. *Party and Ideology in the United States Congress*. Lanham, MD: University Press of America.

Sharkansky, Ira. 1970. *The Routines of Politics*. New York: Van Nostrand Reinhold.

Shuman, Michael. 1990. "What the Framers Really Said About Foreign Policy Powers." *Intergovernmental Perspective* 16: 27–31.

Sloss, James, and James Kneafsey. 1977. "The Demand for Intercity Rail Travel: A Comparison of the British and American Experience." *Transportation Journal* 16: 71–80.

Smith, Steven, and Christopher Deering. 1984. *Committees in Congress*. Washington, DC: CQ Press.

Smith, Zachary. 1986. "Review of Martin Melosi's *Coping with Abundance: Energy and Environment in Industrial America*." *Social Science Quarterly* 67: 461–462.

Statistical Abstract. Annual. Washington, DC: Bureau of the Census.

Statistical Appendix to Amtrak FY 1994 Annual Report. 1994. Washington, DC: National Railroad Passenger Corporation.

Stephenson, Frederick. 1987. *Transportation USA*. Reading, MA: Addison-Wesley.

Stover, John. 1961. *American Railroads*. Chicago: University of Chicago.

———. 1970. *The Life and Decline of the American Railroad*. New York: Oxford.

Talley, Wayne. 1983. *Introduction to Transportation*. Cincinnati: South-Western.

U.S. Crude Oil, Natural Gas, and Natural Gas Liquids Reserves: 1986 Annual Report. 1987. Washington, DC: Energy Information Administration.

U.S. Passenger Rail Technologies. 1983. Washington, DC: Office of Technology Assessment, OTA-STI-222.

Van Fleet, James. 1956. *Rail Transport and the Winning of Wars*. Washington, DC: Association of American Railroads.

Walker, Jack. 1969. "The Diffusion of Innovations Among the American States." *American Political Science Review* 63: 880–899.

———. 1971. "Innovation in State Politics." In *Politics in the American States*, 2nd ed., edited by Herbert Jacob and Kenneth Vines. Boston: Little, Brown, 354–387.

Weaver, R. Kent. 1985. *The Politics of Industrial Change*. Washington, DC: Brookings.

Webley, Simon. 1985. *Stiffening the Sinews of the Nations*. London: British–North American Committee.

Wildavsky, Aaron. 1988. *The New Politics of the Budgetary Process*. Glenview, IL: Scott, Foresman.

———. 1974. *The Politics of the Budgetary Process*, 2nd ed. Boston: Little, Brown.

Wilner, Frank. 1994. *The Amtrak Story*. Omaha: Simmons-Boardman.

Wilson, Rick. 1986. "An Empirical Test of Preferences for the Political Pork Barrel: District Level Appropriations for River and Harbor Legislation, 1889–1913." *American Journal of Political Science* 30: 725–754.

Wonnacott, Ronald, and Thomas Wonnacott. 1979. *Econometrics*, 2nd ed. New York: Wiley.

World Almanac. Annual. New York: Newspaper Enterprise Association.

Wright, Gerald, Robert Erikson, and John McIver. 1985. "Measuring State Partisanship and Ideology with Survey Data." *Journal of Politics* 47: 469–489.

———. 1987. "Public Opinion and Policy Liberalism in the American States." *American Journal of Political Science* 31: 980–1001.

Zimmerman, Karl. 1981. *Amtrak at Milepost 10*. Park Forest, IL: PTJ Publishing.

Index

About the Book

David Nice reviews the circumstances, expectations, and politics that led to the creation of a national passenger rail system out of what had been a myriad of struggling private services.

The book begins with a discussion of the various challenges that Amtrak faced when it was developed over twenty years ago. Nice covers the complex politics behind decisions about the reach and frequency of Amtrak service, as well as the fiscal issues involved in the railroad's continuing attempts to modernize its equipment. He examines the different roles of U.S. national and state governments in subsidizing Amtrak; the factors that have contributed to the wide, year-to-year variance in the system's ridership and financial performance; and the uneven results of Amtrak's experiments with international service. Noting that the system faces continued criticism and threat from a variety of sources, Nice concludes with an evaluation of how Amtrak fits with the nation's overall transportation needs.

David C. Nice is professor of political science at Washington State University. He is author of *Policy Innovation in State Government* and *Federalism: The Politics of Intergovernmental Relations*.